Y2K and Y-O-U

THE REAL GOODS SOLAR LIVING BOOKS

←——→

Wind Power for Home & Business: Renewable Energy for the 1990s and Beyond
by Paul Gipe

The Independent Home: Living Well with Power from the Sun, Wind, and Water
by Michael Potts

*Real Goods Solar Living Sourcebook: The Complete Guide to Renewable Energy
Technologies and Sustainable Living,* Ninth Edition, edited by John Schaeffer

The Straw Bale House by Athena Swentzell Steen, Bill Steen,
and David Bainbridge, with David Eisenberg

The Rammed Earth House by David Easton

The Real Goods Independent Builder: Designing & Building a House Your Own Way
by Sam Clark

The Passive Solar House: Using Solar Design to Heat and Cool Your Home
by James Kachadorian

A Place in the Sun: The Evolution of the Real Goods Solar Living Center
by John Schaeffer and the Collaborative Design/Construction Team

Hemp Horizons: The Comeback of the World's Most Promising Plant
by John W. Roulac

Mortgage-Free! Radical Strategies for Home Ownership by Rob Roy

The Earth-Sheltered House: An Architect's Sketchbook by Malcolm Wells

Wind Energy Basics: A Guide to Small and Micro Wind Systems by Paul Gipe

Y2K and Y-O-U: The Sane Person's Home-Preparation Guide
by Dermot McGuigan and Beverly Jacobson

Real Goods Trading Company in Ukiah, California, was founded in 1978 to make available new tools to help people live self-sufficiently and sustainably. Through seasonal catalogs, a periodical (*The Real Goods News*), a bi-annual *Solar Living Sourcebook*, as well as retail outlets, Real Goods provides a broad range of tools for independent living.

"Knowledge is our most important product" is the Real Goods motto. To further its mission, Real Goods has joined with Chelsea Green Publishing Company to co-create and co-publish the Real Goods Solar Living Book series. The titles in this series are written by pioneering individuals who have firsthand experience in using innovative technology to live lightly on the planet. Chelsea Green books are both practical and inspirational, and they enlarge our view of what is possible as we enter the next millennium.

Stephen Morris
President, Chelsea Green

John Schaeffer
President, Real Goods

Y2K AND Y-O-U

The Sane Person's Home-Preparation Guide

Dermot McGuigan
and Beverly Jacobson

CHELSEA GREEN PUBLISHING COMPANY
White River Junction, Vermont
Totnes, England

Designed by Dede Cummings.

Disclaimer: This book is meant to educate. It is not intended to be used as an alternative to skilled professionals such as your electrician, plumber, and other experts. Any application of the ideas described in the book are at the reader's discretion, and neither the authors nor the publisher assume any responsibility of liability therefor. While every effort has been made to present the information in the book as accurately as possible, ongoing research and the constant flow of new information may change or even invalidate some of the ideas and data in the book.

Printed in the United States of America.

03 02 01 00 99   1 2 3 4 5

First printing, February 1999.

♾ This book is printed on 60# Rolland Opaque, 20 percent PCF (process chlorine free) post-consumer waste, acid-free paper.

Library of Congress Cataloging-in-Publication Data
McGuigan, Dermot, 1949–
      Y2K and Y-O-U : the sane person's home-preparation guide /
Dermot McGuigan and Beverly Jacobson.
         p.   cm. — (Real Goods solar living book)
ISBN 1–890132–26–8 (alk. paper)
        1. Year 2000 date conversion (Computer systems) 2. Home
economics. I. Jacobson, Beverly, 1927–   . II. Title.
III. Series.
OA76. 76. S64M38   1999
005. 1'6—dc21   99–11628
                                                              CIP

Chelsea Green books may be purchased for educational, business, or advocacy use. For information about bulk discounts, please contact the sales manager at the address below.

Chelsea Green Publishing Company
P.O. Box 428
White River Junction, Vermont 05001
telephone (800) 639-4099
www.chelseagreen.com

For Lyman Wood,
who showed so many

*to unite
avocation and vocation
as two eyes make one in sight . . .*

➤ CONTENTS

ACKNOWLEDGMENTS

We are deeply grateful to the following people, without whom this book would be less than it is, or would not be at all:

To Dr. Douglass Carmichael for his generous spirit and his wise eagle-eye view of Y2K and the nature of complex systems;

To Marsha McGuigan for her constant support;

To Karen Moore for her boundless enthusiasm, attention to detail, and valuable research;

To Frances Williams for her enthusiasm and creative questions, and her writing and organizing skills;

To Steve Moore, architect, for his most valuable feedback and insight;

To Don Schroeder, master electrician, for "grounding" some of this book;

To Kristin Camp and Alan Berolzheimer, for their excellent editorial help;

Special thanks to Doug Pratt of Real Goods and Kirk Herander of Vermont Solar Engineering.

INTRODUCTION

It's a major problem.

JOHN KOSKINEN, *Council Chair of the President's Council on the Year 2000 Conversion, 60 Minutes, November 29, 1998*

The Year 2000 problem is a specific threat deserving immediate attention. Clearly, there is nothing hypothetical about this problem—we know that it is coming and we know when—and its effects will be far- and wide-ranging in both the private sector and the government.

SAM NUNN, *former U.S. Senator from Georgia in testimony before the Judiciary Subcommittee on Technology, Terrorism, and Government Information, March 17, 1998*

HOW WILL THE YEAR 2000 computer problem affect your home? No one knows for sure, but many government and industry leaders are telling us to be prepared. They warn that there may be intermittent power failures, disruptions in the delivery of heating fuel, difficulties with the food and water supply, and breakdowns in sanitation services. President Clinton pointed out in July 1998 that Y2K "could affect electric power, phone service, air travel, and major governmental service."

Of course, if such disruptions occur, they could be a blessing in disguise, for they may turn Y2K into a new opportunity—to change our lifestyles in the direction of simplicity and away from the high-tech developments that have created our dependence on computers.

What is this Year 2000 problem? Also known as Y2K or the millennium bug, the issue stems from a tiny misjudgment that occurred half a century ago. When computers were new and memory was expensive, programmers decided to designate the year with two digits instead of four in order to save space—for example, 1965 was coded as "65." They wrote software that assumed every year began with 19 and neglected to anticipate the year 2000. The programmers expected, of course, that the early versions of software they were using would quickly become obsolete. But, in a curious twist of electronic fate, software has turned out to be a different kind of technology than toasters, cars, or television sets. When a new version of a program is developed, the earlier version does not disappear; instead it is built upon, with new material added as needed. Thus the flawed programs were replicated by each successive generation. Today there are billions of lines of computer code, many of which contain date errors, and more than 25 billion embedded microprocessors, of which an estimated .5 to 2 percent have incorrect date information. Some industries, such as health care and electric supply, have higher concentrations of "date-sensitive" embedded chips.

Back in the 1970s, when microprocessors first appeared, designers of embedded systems fell in love with them because one tiny microchip, plus a little code, could replace hundreds of previously used instructions. They were also very cheap. Ease of use and cost effectiveness made microprocessors and embedded chips ubiquitous, turning up in coffee makers, talking toys, thermostats, air conditioners, television sets, VCRs, cars, elevators, streetlights, automatic doors, airplanes, airplane control systems, and the national power grid. They regulate many functions of refineries, oil and gas pipelines, power generation plants, power distribution systems, food distribution systems, telecommunications, and water and sewage treatment plants. Even if only one percent of these embedded microprocessors contain date errors and fail to read the year 2000 accurately, that may be enough to cause computers to shut down the systems they control, or to spew out faulty data. Together with errors in lines of code, these embedded microprocessors are at the root of the Year 2000 dilemma.

Is this problem fixable? Of course, but it is complex and time consuming. Programmers must rewrite the software; to do that they need to review it line by line, which can be done relatively easily but takes time, money, and labor. However, some experts say that software is only 20 percent of the Year 2000 problem; date-sensitive embedded processors make up the other 80 percent. After they fix the software, technicians must tackle the hardware, correcting it by inserting a semiconductor clock chip that is Year 2000-compliant. This replacement part must be compatible with other embedded chips within the same system. To complicate matters further, it is often difficult to locate the embedded processors, and some of them are hard to access, such as those under the ocean at off-shore drilling rigs, or those encased in steel, or buried in concrete.

Your home may be up-to-date and efficient, with more computer power in it than the entire MIT campus had twenty years ago, but what about its link with the world out there that services your light switch, furnace, phone, water system, and stove? After all, these are the essentials that make your home thoroughly livable. Thanks to America's extremely efficient electric power industry, well-protected underground gas lines, a phone service second to none, and automatic fuel delivery, we simply take for granted the delivery of services when we need them and let our homes purr along on their own. However, extending unseen from your home lies a vast, complex grid of high-tech connections powered by computers. This grid projects throughout and beyond America into countries that supply us with much of the fuel that runs our electric power plants and heats our homes. If this interconnected, computer-controlled grid does not work properly, the steady supply of services may be disrupted, and your home may become unlivable.

Computer glitches involving the year 2000 have already occurred, according to the Cassandra Project, a citizen's group devoted to increasing Y2K awareness. In April 1998, the computer network that schedules patient appointments at three hospitals and seventy-five clinics in Pennsylvania shut down—all because one person punched in an appointment for January 2000. Royal Sutherland Hospital in New South Wales has identified two processors, a laser camera, and an ultrasound machine that will become inoperable on January 1, 2000. Closer to home, several Diamond Shamrock gas stations in Boulder County, Colorado, are not able to accept credit cards with "00" as an expiration date. The clerk has to punch in the card number manually and set the expiration date to "99." Considerably more ominous is what happened last fall at a Phillips Petroleum Company oil and gas production platform in the North Sea.

When engineers ran Year 2000 tests, an essential safety system for detecting harmful gases such as hydrogen sulfide became confused and shut down. This was just a simulation. In real life, the platform would have been rendered unusable, disrupting the oil and gas supply of the company and, down the line, of local businesses that rely on Phillips products.

This does not surprise us. In fact, we may be in for trouble before the millennium arrives. Some programmers expect surprises on September 9, 1999, because 09/09/99 has often been used by programmers as a default date setting. There is no reliable information on what this may or may not do, only opinions. But the very fact that the 1999 fiscal year begins for the federal government on April 1, and for most of the states on September 1 or October 1, gives one pause. When these fiscal years kick in, the computers involved will bring the following twelve months into their systems, which may trigger all the computer bugs and embedded chip problems we thought we would not face until January 1, 2000. Rumor abounds, and no clear information is available as of this writing.

As if that were not enough, welcome to the February 2000 surprise. In the sixteenth century, a Jesuit mathematician made a calculation that could affect our lives in 2000. To make human time coincide with astronomical dictates, he decided that every fourth century should be a leap year. The year 2000 will be the very first time that this rule applies. Unfortunately, not many programmers were aware of this. Now the question is—which programmers knew about it, and which ones did not? Which programs concur with the leap year and which do not? When computers that recognize 2000 as a leap year shake hands with those that do not, will the exchange of information be affected by a dispute as to what day it is? What will happen to the computers that run our basic infrastructure if this inability to agree corrupts data? Many experts believe that a disagreement affecting such a basic principle will cause computers that contradict each other to disengage, which will interrupt the flow of essential services.

Lack of hard information on the true level of Y2K readiness creates a vacuum that is all too easily filled with fear. Fear creates its own cloud of reaction, which can, in turn, cause genuine shortages, sometimes exceeding any real potential for hardship. Hollywood is adding to the problem by scheduling several disaster movies featuring the millennium bug for release in 1999. Charles Mackay published his classic book *Extraordinary Popular Delusions and the Madness of Crowds* in 1841, which describes a series of delusions that swept through previously sensible populations that suddenly fell victim to inflated hopes and fears. A century and a half later we humans are just as susceptible to panics based on misinformation. There is an ocean of opinion published on the World Wide Web and in print that is simply not grounded in fact. The truth is that, while Y2K is a real problem, the world will not end on January 1, 2000.

Dr. Douglass Carmichael, one of the nation's premier thinkers on Y2K, is calling for a National Y2K Center, similar to the Centers for Disease Control, financed by the government as a world resource, which would take responsibility for technology, and make available the best perspectives, and the best facts. Says Carmichael:

> I find myself in anguish over the lack of good facts. Facts have to be stories that tell us what is known about propagation of errors in interconnected systems, and remediation techniques that have worked, not abstract configurations, but detailed examples of assessment, remediation, and testing. Such a center would have high visibility, the support of the President and Congressional committees, and would give us much better assessments than we have now. If we had even several good case studies of how a major organization took on Y2K, the educational value would be a full order of magnitude more important and helpful than our present approach. Those who are lagging would be galvanized by such leadership, combined with explicit detailed case studies here and around the globe. The world needs leadership on Y2K and the time is now.

This book will tell you how to safeguard your home from a variety of failures—electricity, fuel, food, water, and sanitation. With backup systems in place, you can live in relative comfort if the power grid fails, fuel supplies do not arrive at their proper distribution points, or food stays in warehouses. The concept we are promoting is that of resilience—of creating backup systems that can be used in an emergency to provide for the basic needs of your home. Along the way, you may be inspired to create an independent home, one that can provide for all its own energy needs on an everyday basis, and the strategies we suggest will take you in that direction.

Of course you are asking why you might need to establish resilience. It is an excellent question, particularly since it is tempting to regard Y2K as a non-issue, because we have no reference point—never in human history have we experienced such a situation. Moreover, it is difficult to think that computers will fail; we have become accustomed to the many ways they have made our lives quicker and easier for several decades. Only if you have lived through a natural disaster—a blizzard, ice storm, hurricane, or earthquake—do you know how hard it can be to stay in a home without light or heat or water or the ability to cook. Since these natural disasters are infrequent, we tend to remain complacent because we do not think it will happen to us. Even after experiencing a power failure, many people do not buy into backup systems.

In January 1998, a major ice storm affected northern New England and much of eastern Canada. More than three million people were affected by the power outage, most for a relatively short period of time. Tens of thousands of people were totally unprepared, some going without power for six weeks, scrambling for generators or gathering together around a fireplace that seemed to draw more heat up the chimney than it radiated into the room. About thirty thousand people sought refuge in shelters, and an untold number stayed in hotels or with friends and family.

We live in northern Vermont, and we conducted an informal survey of some friends and neighbors: Only two families out of twenty-three had continued to live comfortably during the ice storm, actually enjoying the peace and quiet of their enforced retreat. They had resilient homes with backup heating and cooking systems; one family had a generator. Eleven families experienced a range of inconveniences, some worse than others. It was not an experience they would choose to repeat. The remaining ten families needed to find refuge elsewhere for at least part of the time. Of the twenty-one families who had problems during the ice storm, only three have taken subsequent steps to create backup systems.

We may be in danger of the same kind of denial with Y2K. As president of the Information Association of America Harris N. Miller said, "If the year 2000 had a national bird, it would be the ostrich." John L. Petersen and his co-authors of *The Year 2000: Social Chaos or Social Transformation?* explain that Americans have "great collective faith in technology. We can't see the extent of our interconnectedness. We only see the interdependencies when the relationships are disrupted."

How Serious Is The Millennium Bug?

No one knows how serious the millennium bug will be. Some alarmists predict a total meltdown of society. These are the folks who are moving to the hills. At the other end of the spectrum are people who insist there is no problem, and if there is, the government and private industry, large and small, will solve it in plenty of time for January 1, 2000.

There is a middle ground, however, where most reasonable people stand. This point of view recognizes that there may be a problem, accepts the fact that we do not know how severe it will be, and prepares reasonably to meet any challenge. This is where we stand. We believe in hoping for the best but preparing, if not for the worst, then for something in between. Because there may be interruptions in some services, we show you how protect your home with minimal expense and effort. What is more, all of our suggestions are applicable to natural disasters as well as to Y2K. We believe this is a practical and easy approach to a situation that may turn out to be huge, medium-sized, or highly overrated. Our motto: Being ready for the unknown is a very smart way to be.

Peter de Jager (www.year2000.com), one of the most knowledgeable computer gurus in the country, has been beating the Y2K drum for almost a decade trying to spread awareness of the problem. He says, "Will we fix everything? Of course not. But I honestly believe the mission-critical stuff will get done. And where it doesn't get done, work-arounds can, and will, be found." He goes on to say that we should never forget "our well-proven ability to overcome adversity." So don't head for the hills. Be smart and turn your house into a Y2K-prepared home. Then, instead of being part of the problem, you will be part of the solution.

What Do We Mean By A Y2K Prepared Home?

We all live in a chain of linked interdependencies and it's sensible to have realistic expectations about whether the services we depend on, which come to us from great distances, will be available 100 percent of the time. If there is a chance that they will not, we should make adequate provision for potential shortfalls. We are suggesting a series of simple steps that can make your home ready for any Y2K disruptions, a short staircase of possibilities. Some may apply to your particular home and some may not. After you select the ones that will make your home livable during an emergency, you can use your time to research, buy, and install these options, and plan so that these improvements fall within your budget.

With a prepared home, you can continue to live in relative comfort even if prolonged interruptions of essential services occur. You will not be entirely dependent upon a supply of remotely generated electricity; on municipal systems for drinking water and sanitation; on a well-stocked supermarket; and on local gas, coal, or oil companies to deliver fuel for heating and cooking. Equally important, you will be relatively immune to the stress and fear that may arise if supplies are delayed or interrupted. For example, one homeowner lost heat, water, and sump pump for about seven days during the 1998 ice storm. He watched as the temperature inside his home fell to 34° Fahrenheit and the water level in the basement rose. His home was within hours of freezing solid when a friendly plumber lent him a generator. Imagine how stressed you would be in that situation. We invite you to take control of your home and create a series of backup systems.

Y2K and Y-O-U describes how you can take thoughtful steps, at a reasonable cost, so that your home life will not become a burden as the result of interrupted services. With this book you can create a home that is ready for almost anything, a resilient home that happily uses electric utilities and other services when they are available but can function independently when they are not—truly a win–win situation.

Our goal is to encourage resilience, not survivalism; community involvement, not isolationism. Unlike some families in our informal survey, the great ice storm of 1998 was our awakening call—one disaster was enough for us. We considered the needs of our respective homes, the heating and cooling systems, and the most cost-effective ways to back up these systems. We gave careful thought to our food, water, sanitation, health, and lighting needs, and determined a variety of solutions that would provide them in an emergency. We considered how we could reach out to our neighbors and the larger community, how we could encourage our communities to prepare, and how we could help our neighbors in times of crisis as well.

As we worked through this process, it became clear that while each home and family (and community) has the same basic requirements, these needs can be met with a wide variety of solutions. The method you choose will depend upon your home's unique circumstances, as well as your own creativity, personal preference, values, and budget. We encourage you to keep the environmental impact of your decisions in mind. Although these solutions are applicable to any natural disaster, this book does not have complete instructions regarding flood, earthquake, or hurricane preparedness. That information is available from your state government or from the Federal Emergency Management Administration (FEMA). We invite you to explore the simple ideas that can turn your existing home into a Y2K-resilient one: a home that you can continue to live in and enjoy during a temporary or even prolonged disruption of essential services. Each chapter considers a number of options to meet a basic need of your home.

Chapter 1 explains how Y2K may disrupt the supply of electricity to your home, and why regional power failures may occur intermittently throughout the year 2000 and beyond. It also tells how the British government managed power disruptions in Britain during the 1970s, making them predictable and of limited duration in any given area.

Chapter 2 encourages the use of solar and wind power as Earth-friendly ways to meet your electrical needs. We discuss generators, and give some important tips about choosing one and increasing its efficiency with a battery/inverter system or load-shedding device. We also describe safe methods of fuel storage. Read this chapter before you rush out to buy a gas-fueled generator, as there may be better options for your family.

Chapter 3 discusses ways to heat without electricity, using renewable resources. As many of us have learned the hard way, even an oil or gas furnace usually requires electricity to operate. Wind, ice, and snow can create havoc with power lines. By preparing for Y2K, you will be ready for other emergencies as well. The chapter includes tips on insulating your home and on using the Sun's rays coming through your windows as an additional source of heat. Our preference and emphasis is on heating with renewable energy and locally available resources, such as solar energy and wood. The new, more efficient woodstoves make less work for the homeowner, and greatly reduce environmental pollution. By choosing renewable energy as a backup, you will not only create a resilient home, you will be on your way to developing an independent home, as well.

Chapter 4 talks about ways that you can heat with propane, natural gas, and oil that do not require electricity. We consider Y2K's potential effect on the availability of these fuels, since shortages may last into the year 2000 and beyond, and recommend ways to store these fuels safely.

Chapter 5 considers your home's cooling needs. During hot weather, the demand for electricity sometimes outstrips the local utility's ability to supply it, and power has to be diverted from other areas. When you add Y2K to this already strained situation, power shortages may occur during the summer of 2000 and beyond. Your air conditioner or fan may not work when you need it the most. Passive cooling methods can lessen the amount of heat entering your home, and eliminate or reduce your need for home-generated electricity. You will be ready for power outages caused by summer storms as well.

Chapter 6 explains why "just in time" delivery of food to the supermarket may become a problem because of delays caused by Y2K. Rather than hoarding food in a panic, we advise preparing a pantry for everyday use during food shortages, as our farming ancestors did to get through the winter before there were supermarkets. We give advice on buying and storing grocery items and prepackaged meals. We invite you to explore the joys and benefits of gardening, or buying "shares" in local CSA (community supported agriculture) farms.

Chapter 7 considers water and sanitation needs. In addition to discussing the safe storage of water, and emergency methods of obtaining and treating water, we look at hand pumps that will work for deep wells; solar- and wind-generated electricity to run your well pump; and innovative collection systems for water. We also give examples of how some community municipal water and sanitation systems are preparing for Y2K, and invite you to talk with your community's leaders.

Chapter 8 encourages you to be pro-active in caring for your health needs, in the event that Y2K disrupts the health care delivery system. We give advice on dealing with stress before and during disruptions in essential services.

Chapter 9 talks briefly about banking, financial services, home computers, home appliances, transportation issues, and communications.

Chapter 10 discusses the importance of developing connections in your local neighborhood and in the larger community. We cover ways to talk to your neighbors about Y2K without alarming them, and techniques to encourage your municipal leaders to act. The chapter contains examples of communities working together to be ready for Y2K.

Chapter 11 compares the cost of preparing a Y2K-ready home with the cost of doing nothing. We also offer three case studies of resilient homes.

It may be that, after you have read a chapter, your imagination will be sparked, and you will discover a new and completely different way to meet your family's needs. We invite you to share your creative ideas with us so that we may include them in future editions of this book.

Y2K as Opportunity

The crisis brought on by Y2K gives us an opportunity to reassess how we are living our lives. Chances are that your home and family depend upon distant essential services over which you have no control. While dependence on regional and national services and products has its benefits, it also has its costs. Many of these costs are hidden, or so far removed from our awareness that we tend to forget them.

If, for example, you were able to observe a local farmer spraying pesticides and herbicides on his crops, and then washing carefully for fear of poisoning his children when he returned home, you would undoubtably think twice about buying his produce. Yet every day, millions of Americans buy imported or long-distance produce without knowing what chemicals they contain. Other associated costs include the pollution of our ground-water, the diseases inflicted upon those who pick the sprayed crops, the massive amounts of irreplaceable fossil fuel needed to transport the produce over long distances, the assault on the Earth in obtaining and using the fossil fuel, the soil erosion caused by modern corporate farming, and the ultimate effect of all this on the nation's health. Finally, consider the waste and cost of spoiled food—because, when the produce has sat too long in the warehouse, the truck or railroad car, the supermarket, or our refrigerators, it is thrown out.

There is something very sensible and rewarding about the home and lifestyle that gathers what is needed from within the local area, and contributes in turn to a vibrant local economy and community life. You can augment this lifestyle by cultivating your own garden, or buying "shares" in community supported agriculture. When you support local agriculture, you have more awareness and control over how the produce you eat is grown, and you can avoid the hidden costs by supporting Earth-friendly methods of agriculture. Also, if you are like us, you are less likely to waste any of the produce in which you have invested your time and labor. If you have too much, you will give some away, or "put by" the excess for later use.

As you read this book, and consider the various ways to create backup systems for your home, we invite you to keep a wider view in mind. There are a number of different ways to prepare your home for Y2K. You can create minimal emergency backup systems, and that will be a good start on a resilient home. You can also use the opportunity of Y2K to make long-term changes in your home. By reducing your home's energy needs, by choosing renewable energy, by participating in community supported agriculture, by using water resources carefully, by reducing waste and pollution, and by living a healthy lifestyle, you can help make a difference in our world.

CHAPTER 1

DISRUPTIONS IN ELECTRICITY AND FUEL SUPPLY

How and Why They May Occur

I expect we will have brownouts and regional blackouts;
in some areas of the country there will be power failures.

SENATOR BOB BENNETT,
*chairman of the U.S. Senate Special Committee
on the Year 2000 Technology Problem,
speaking to the National Press Club, July 15, 1998*

 THE ENERGY SUPPLIED TO YOUR HOME,
whether it is natural or propane gas, heating oil, or
electricity, is dependent upon a complex tapestry of
services. A Y2K weakness in one area may affect other
areas as well. With the millennium bug, you may not
see anything as dramatic as high-voltage electric pylons
collapsing, as they did during the northeast ice storm of January 1998,
but the effect on your home could be the same. In this chapter, we explain why our nation's electricity grid is vulnerable to Y2K, and why the
problems may last well into the year 2000 and beyond. We caution
against relying on promises that the electric industry will be Y2K-com-
pliant in time, given the uncertainties that abound less than a year before
the new millennium arrives. Finally, we explain why disruptions may occur in the delivery of heating fuel to your home and encourage you to
create resilient backup systems.

Why the Electric Grid is Vulnerable

The interconnectedness of the power grid makes it both strong and vulnerable. Strong, because regional power systems can direct electricity from one area to another as needed. Vulnerable, because a problem in one area can sometimes cause a chain reaction, resulting in a "crash" affecting large numbers of people. For example, a small transmission relay that was incorrectly set at a single generating plant in Ontario caused the great East Coast blackout of 1965. Within minutes, the wrong setting tripped an entire system, and Ontario, New England, and New York were blacked out. The Y2K flaw is like seeding the power grid with multiple incorrectly set relay switches. (See the Introduction for an explanation of the Y2K computer and embedded chip flaw.)

Another example of how the interconnectedness of the grid increases its vulnerability occurred on August 10, 1996, when the power system in the western United States went down because of trees that had grown into a transmission line. Four million people in nine states were left without power. After the outage, Marcie Edwards, director of bulk power at the Los Angeles Department of Water and Power, said that utilities needed to share technical information; she urged that, just because companies had moved away from sharing financial information, their operational divisions needed "to cooperate more closely in the future to avoid such disturbances." Since this statement, it appears that the drift toward separating the various functions of the electric utility infrastructure has continued, resulting in less coordination. Utilities are selling off their power plants to other utilities and independent power providers.

It is not just faulty equipment and vegetation that we must worry about. Bad weather is notorious for causing power outages. In 1997, the New York City area lost power for about twenty-five hours, partially due to lightning strikes. The great ice storm of January 1998 left millions without power, some for up to six weeks. A December 1998 ice storm in the Southeast left 600,000 people without power, some for over a week.

Electric Utilities and their Vendors

Even if the electric power industry became Y2K-compliant in time, the companies that the power industry depends on may not be ready. For example, power distribution depends on telecommunications for planning, coordination, and dispatch. Functioning telecommunication in turn depends on electric power and satellites. To their credit, the utility industry has included the need to diversify their communications as part of their contingency plan.

Most of America's electricity comes from generating plants powered by fossil fuels, without which they cannot continue to operate. Utilities do stockpile some fuel in reserve for storms and other disruptions. But the availability of fossil fuel depends upon the interlinked industries of drilling, refining, and transportation—all highly dependent on computers and therefore vulnerable to Y2K. Even if all parts of the fossil fuel industry were Y2K-compliant, we would still have a problem because 50 percent of our oil is imported. Many of the countries that sell oil to the United States have been slow to become aware of Y2K and are unlikely to fix all their systems in time. As for propane, 40 percent comes from oil refining and 11 percent is imported.

Within the last twenty-five years, power plants have developed a cost-efficient, heavily computer-dependent "just in time" inventory system for fuel. In most regions of the country, a locally available supply of liquid propane or oil for home heating will last for about seven days, on average. Power plants depend on uninterrupted fuel deliveries. What will happen if fuel does not arrive? Some experts caution that regional power outages may occur intermittently throughout the year 2000; inadequate fuel may be on hand to meet peak demand during the summer cooling season.

Y2K Fixes in the Power Industry May Not Happen in Time

All power plants have control rooms that use computers and software, and many power plants have control functions that use embedded chips. The industry is working hard to become Y2K-compliant before the year 2000 but this may not happen in time. For example, in November 1998,

Britain's United Utilities became the first power company to admit publicly that essential services could fail because of Y2K problems. They said, "Despite our best efforts, there remains a risk of failure of systems." United Utilities has achieved considerable success in preparing for Y2K; they have checked all of their embedded systems and believe they are compliant. But the company is aware that they may have overlooked chips or errors in computer code somewhere in the system. This is simple reality—no one can give a 100 percent guarantee that electricity will continue to flow without interruption.

In September 1998, the North American Electric Reliability Council (NERC) issued its report, "Preparing the Electric Power Systems of North America for Transition to the Year 2000." The report's bottom line is that NERC is "cautiously optimistic" regarding the utilities' capacity to supply uninterrupted electricity. "Cautiously optimistic" means that they hope for the best but cannot guarantee you will have electricity when 2000 arrives. The report says that the pace of remediation work "must be accelerated in order to bring utilities into Y2K compliance." NERC also advises electricity customers to "think about the impact of Y2K on your business or home" and to "seek information and guidance from your local electricity supplier regarding what steps you should be taking, if any, regarding power supplies." Keep in mind that this is only a preliminary assessment. Still, these are not totally comforting words.

While parts of the power industry are reportedly making gallant efforts to fix their systems in time, smaller municipal and cooperative electric systems have been slow to address the Y2K situation, which adds to the problem. Then there are the ostriches. For example, when we spoke early in 1998 to the general manager of a Canadian power plant owned by an international independent power company, we discovered that he was completely unaware of Y2K and that his head office had not provided him with any information about Y2K.

Nuclear Power Plants in Question

A vulnerable link in the electricity supply system is nuclear power, which provides approximately 22 percent of electric power in the United States. Despite the use of older analog technology for core function, on average a nuclear power plant depends on more than three hundred computer software programs and thousands of embedded microprocessor controls. This is not the best situation, particularly since parts of the country, such as the East Coast and New England, depend upon nuclear power for as much as 35 percent of their local electricity.

The Nuclear Regulatory Commission (NRC) will require written verification of Y2K-compliance by July 1, 1999; non-compliant plants will not be allowed to operate until they meet NRC standards. This should ensure public safety, but shutting down nuclear power plants will cause electricity shortages. As of this writing, not a single nuclear plant in the U.S. is Y2K-compliant.

In October 1998, the NRC made available its audit of the Monticello nuclear power plant, owned by Northern States Power Company in Minnesota. Monticello started an ad hoc evaluation of some of the plant's computer systems in 1997 and implemented its formal Y2K program in June 1998, later than most nuclear plants. The NRC reports that Monticello is still in the initial assessment phase and that its Y2K team is "undertaking an ambitious schedule in order to meet the July 1999 Y2K readiness date established by the NRC." The NRC considers Monticello's schedule to be achievable even though there are 290 software items at the site, and of the 453 embedded chips that have been identified, 150 still need attention. A significant item in the report is that Monticello has not begun contingency planning and will not do so until January 1999. That is awfully late, in view of the uncertainty that Monticello will meet its "ambitious" deadline.

The NRC has recently issued audit reports on four other nuclear plants. One will be three months late meeting the NRC's July 1 deadline, two others will be a month or so late with part of their plan, and the fourth is ". . . accepting vendor certifications for embedded components including those in high priority mission critical systems without conducting additional . . . testing at the plant." Since no one can guarantee that you will have electricity when 2000 dawns, prepare resilient backup systems for your home to carry you through until problems are resolved. The next chapter discusses some options.

Brownouts and Blackouts

Many people are concerned about interruptions in domestic heating fuel supplies because of transportation and refining problems. Let's examine the difficulties facing the electrical utilities and the infrastructure that delivers oil, propane, and natural gas to homes and businesses.

The good news is that many older fossil fuel plants operating on coal, oil, or gas use analog instead of digital control functions. These plants are not subject to embedded chip problems and therefore should function as long as they can get a steady supply of fuel. As an added bonus, virtually all fossil fuel-powered electric generating stations have manual overrides. If a remote computerized control unit shuts down a pump or a valve, a worker can override it manually, bringing power back online.

These manual overrides mean that a nationwide blackout is highly unlikely. However, Senator Bob Bennett, who chairs the U.S. Senate Special Committee on the Year 2000 Technology Problem, has expressed concern about brownouts, regional blackouts, and rolling blackouts (scheduled interruptions in power), and many other industry experts have expressed similar concerns. The real issue here is how these events could affect you and your home.

In recent years, electricity supply systems, including reserve systems, have been strained by the demands placed upon them. For example, during a recent bout of hot weather in the Northeast, some utilities asked consumers to turn off their air conditioners and to conserve energy in other ways. This allowed the utility to meet demand without having to use high-priced, polluting resources. While Y2K glitches are unlikely to make the whole grid collapse, they may place an additional burden on an already stressed situation, and regional disruptions may become more likely.

The term brownout describes a drop in utility line voltage. Brownouts occur in areas where power plants supplying the grid cannot keep up with the demand for electricity. Even under the best of circumstances, the perfect matching of demand and supply from remote power plants is impossible to achieve, so utility planners allow for an acceptable voltage bandwidth within which most home and industrial machines can function adequately. Degraded power quality—meaning brownouts—is a less likely subject of concern. More realistically, we will have power or we won't. In New England, for example, the utilities will shed load instead of creating brownouts. After the January 1998 ice storm, as service was restored to consumers in parts of Quebec, dips and surges in voltage were experienced frequently. This is always a concern when power is restored. Utilities warn customers to shut off appliances following a disruption to help accommodate a smooth return to service.

Rolling blackouts are inconvenient, but tolerable, especially if announced so that people can plan for them. Rolling blackouts were used in Britain during a prolonged coal miners' strike in the early 1970s. A three-day work week was enforced by the ruling Conservative party, both to conserve fuel resources and to meet the limited electrical demand. In addition, the state-owned central electric board implemented a system of scheduled rolling blackouts throughout the entire country.

Each neighborhood and home knew when they would and would not receive electrical power. Typically, a community, would receive power for four hours one evening, and none the next. The result was a system of neighborly planning, during which people would cook in homes that had power one evening, and then move to another home on the subsequent evening, or they would prepare food and do laundry during periods when power was available.

The system worked, and it worked in a fair and civil manner. New England utilities have plans to enact the same scenario should the need arise. This is an equitable and fair way to deal with fuel shortages, or other power supply problems. Rolling blackouts are also an appropriate measure to keep the overall system in synch.

The probability of a blackout across the entire United States is remote. In mid-1998, Senator Bennett pegged the likelihood that there may be some Y2K-related regional blackouts at 40 percent. The advantage of Y2K over a weather-caused blackout is that the grid will be in place, and we will not have to deal with downed wires and poles that need repair. Rolling blackouts can be planned and implemented as needed, until the problems of fuel supply are resolved, or nuclear power plants are made Y2K-compliant.

Promises, Promises

It is easy to explain why the grid is vulnerable to Y2K. What is harder, or near impossible, to explain is the extent of this vulnerability. Most electric utilities say that they are or will be Y2K-compliant on a timely basis, and that the computer bug will not affect their capacity to supply electricity to their customers. But outside experts have said that substantial problems resulting from the Y2K bug exist within the electric utility infrastructure and its interconnected systems. For example, Rick Cowles, director of Year 2000 Industry Solutions, in testimony before the subcommittee on technology of the U.S. House Committee on Science, said on May 14, 1998:

> Based on surveys I've conducted at all levels of industry, my best estimate is that only 60 to 70 percent of the [electric] companies are fully aware of the magnitude of the Y2K issue, and are marshaling the necessary resources to address the issue. While the technology issues surrounding Y2K are well understood, in all functional business areas of the electric utility industry, the scope and breadth of the Y2K problem is just beginning to be acknowledged.

Plenty of information exists that belies the standard utility letters of assurance, such as an article in the March 1998 issue of *Business Electrical World*, which reported that Boston Edison was working on its mission-critical systems first—its billing system, transmission and distribution network, and all applications that affect safety. Quoted in the story was a discouraging statement from the company's vice-president of information services: "It would be great to greet the millennium with all ten systems Y2K-compliant, but that's not possible . . . we're doing all we can." In a January 10, 1999 Boston Globe story, when asked "Will the lights stay on January 1, 2000?" Boston Edison manager Jim Ashkar replied, "That's the $64,000 question! . . . Anybody who assumes it will be perfection has a misperception."

Compare that with the testimony of Maria Nahn, an attorney with Wisconsin Power and Light Company, before the Wisconsin State Assembly's Y2K committee, during which she said that failures of the power and the municipal water systems are likely. Nahn reported that the company is encouraging its customers to look into alternative energy sources, including home generators, in anticipation of Y2K-related power failures. The day after her testimony was reported in the Milwaukee *Journal Sentinel*, a spokesperson for the utility said that Nahn's statements "didn't reflect the advice we are giving our customers."

On December 27, 1998, the *New York Times* reported that New Jersey's Public Service Electric and Gas (PSE&G) has 728 computer programs with 46 million lines of code, written in 27 programming languages. The article states:

> How well they get fixed or replaced could determine whether the lights and heat stay on in New Jersey come January 1, 2000. . . . The bottom line, however, is this: Despite . . . shortcuts, despite budgeting $91.6 million for Y2K work, and despite starting its cleanup more than two years ago—earlier than most utilities—PSE&G will not finish on time. So like many companies, it is resorting to triage, fixing the most important programs first and worrying about minor ones later.

It is comforting that at least one company—United Utilities in England—has had the courage to tell the truth about Y2K. The company is realistic about the extent of the problem, is committed to public disclosure, continues to work hard to become totally Y2K-compliant, and is establishing contingency plans. This is what every public and private power company in the U.S. must do. Perhaps by the time this book is in your hands other utilities will have followed its example.

What is most disturbing is the fact that no one seems to be making contingency plans for Y2K-caused failures. Senator Christopher Dodd, testifying on June 12, 1998, before the U.S. Senate Special Committee on the Year 2000 Technology Problem, said, "I am very, very concerned that even as government and business leaders are finally acknowledging the seriousness of this problem, they are not thinking about the contingency plans that need to be put in place to minimize harm from widespread failures." He has good reason to worry. As Senator John Kyl pointed out in testimony before the same committee on April 23, 1998, "We need serious and well-founded contingency planning for Y2K-related disruptions, to insure, at a minimum, the provision of essential government emergency services." He went on, "When I asked John Koskinen, chairman of the Presidents' Council on Year 2000 Conversion, what the government was doing in the area of contingency planning, he wrote a letter saying that the Federal Emergency Management Agency (FEMA) 'will take the lead in assuring that the federal government is doing all that is necessary to be ready should serious disruptions occur.'" Kyl went on to say he had already written James Lee Witt, FEMA's director, asking about their contingency plans if there are disruptions in the delivery of electricity, and received the following reply from FEMA's assistant director: "FEMA has performed no assessments of the Y2K computer problem on the telecommunications and electric power infrastructures." The letter went on to state "FEMA has no contingency plans" for failures in the electric power industry.

Kyl concluded, "If the agency charged with contingency planning has no contingency plans, then either the Administration does not expect to have any emergency preparedness needs that are Y2K specific, or the federal government is failing in its responsibility to our citizens and needs to correct that deficiency immediately."

This disheartening information makes it imperative that people prepare for emergencies so that they can withstand service disruptions. With an effective backup system in place for your family's heating, cooling, and other energy needs, you can enter the new millennium with confidence and peace of mind.

Fuel for Your Furnace?

Oil drilling, particularly on off-shore platforms and in more remote locations, requires a combination of advanced technology, brute-force engineering, and computing genius. As President Clinton pointed out in 1998, "An oil drilling rig alone may include ten thousand separate chips." Oil refining is a complex chemical process dependent on microprocessors. The transportation of natural gas and oil through pipelines, in tankers, and by truck depends upon computer control rooms and embedded control systems at valve, metering, and distribution stations throughout our national and international fuel distribution grid. The fuel ultimately arrives at a local distribution center, which has its own computers and embedded control systems. Within many homes, heating is supplied at the touch of a thermostat. Under normal conditions, uninterrupted by weather-related problems and the Y2K bug, we remain comfortable.

All the potential Y2K problems regarding fuel imports discussed earlier are equally applicable to domestic heating fuel. Remember the "just in time" inventory system? Well, "just in time" policies could affect the delivery of heating fuel to your home. A local liquid-propane supplier serving nine thousand customers said that at any given time they have enough fuel to last six to eight days. The nearest store of fuel to replenish their supply is 150 miles away. And this source relies in turn upon another distant one. If anyone in this supply setup fails to deliver fuel to the next link in the chain, shortages are inevitable. With all the uncertainties surrounding the year 2000, no one can guarantee that there will not be disruptions in the transportation of fuel.

The electric power grid and the fuel distribution system are vulnerable to disruption even without Y2K. The millennium bug merely amplifies the potential for problems. Intermittent power failures and disruptions in the fuel supply may occur, but these problems can be fixed. They will not last forever. In the meantime, if you follow the advice in the following chapters, you will be well on the way to creating a resilient home.

CHAPTER 2

MEETING YOUR HOME'S ELECTRICAL NEEDS

The United States—with close to half of all computer capacity . . .
—is the world's most advanced and most dependent user of information
technology. Should these systems . . . suffer disruption, it could create a
widespread crisis.

JOEL C. WILLEMSSEN,
Director, Civil Agencies Information Systems,
GAO Testimony, August 19, 1998

I believe that severe disruptions will occur and that they will last perhaps
about a month. Additional problems . . . will continue cropping up
throughout 2000.

Scientific American, *January 19, 1999*

 THE MOST RESILIENT HOME will not need
electricity to function in an emergency, whether that
electricity is home-generated or not. Our core
needs—heating and cooling, cooked food, hot and
cold water, and lighting—can be met without electricity. For heating, you are safer with a passive heating
system such as a woodstove or gas-fueled fireplace insert. Safer, too, is a
home that can be cooled passively without air conditioning. Moving
parts are subject to breakdown, and a generator, furnace, or air conditioner could fail when you need it the most. Similarly, a bottle of water
in hand may be better than two bottles dependent upon a well pump
and generator.

The purpose of this chapter is to discuss electricity needs in the home, and to describe alternative ways in which these needs can be satisfied without using the local electric company. As a matter of fact, almost all needs can be met without electricity. You may choose to have an alternative source of electricity, and our first recommendation is that you consider a renewable energy source, such as solar- or wind-powered electricity. We suggest this choice as either a short-term or a long-term alternative to standby generators powered by fossil fuel, usually gasoline. If a serious interruption in the supply of electricity occurs for any reason, that difficulty may also affect the availability of fuel, rendering a standby generator useless, unless you have a significant store of fuel. We do not recommend storing a lot of gasoline in or near your home. Gasoline is dangerous because it is a fire hazard, and it also poses a threat to the environment, since leaks can enter ground water. But for those who need a reliable source of power for medical reasons, such as diabetics who require a supply of refrigerated insulin twice a day, or the elderly or handicapped, a generator makes sense. It would be best to power it with renewable energy. If you use fossil fuel, propane is the most reliable, because you can store a sufficient quantity safely.

The beauty of a renewable energy system is that it is not dependent upon the vagaries of fuel supply, it represents a healthier, more fundamental shift toward environmentally sound resilience, and it's good for the economy to support what are now mature technologies. Renewable energy is more expensive, but the homeowner can often greatly reduce electric energy requirements through conservation and by installing efficient devices, which are often partially funded by electric utility conservation programs. In the long-term, these savings can offset the upfront cost of renewable electricity. What we are suggesting here is a combined approach to home energy conservation and renewable energy use. You should consider renewable energy not just to enjoy a more secure Y2K experience, but as a development that could be implemented in stages over several years. While all the changes proposed in this book are useful, you are unlikely to complete all of them before December 31, 1999. The best approach would be to make a list of priorities so that your real core needs are satisfied first, but are integrated with a long-term plan. For this approach you can consider electricity produced by a solar system, or a wind generator and a water-pumping windmill.

Whether or not you choose to plan and implement a renewable energy project over time, electricity conservation measures in the home are worthwhile any time. This chapter goes through each of the electrical needs in the home and demonstrates how they can be met with less or no electricity. Next, we discuss different ways to satisfy home electricity requirements.

Household Electrical Needs

In this discussion of different household electrical loads, consider the particulars of your electric system. The truly resilient home needs little, and in many cases, no electricity in order to maintain reasonable comfort in an emergency.

CENTRAL HEATING SYSTEM

All central heating systems require electricity. This reality can be maddening if you experience random electrical outages for whatever reason during the winter heating season. It can lead to feelings of frustration and powerlessness (literally!), particularly when you have a full reserve of home heating fuel that your non-functioning furnace cannot use without electricity to start it. Power outages lasting more than a day create a dividing line between those who can continue to enjoy their homes and those who must leave and find shelter elsewhere until the power comes back on.

Chapters 3 and 4 discuss the merits of electricity-free heating systems, such as wood stoves and space heaters that use fossil fuel, and the need to have a one- or two-month supply of fuel. An electricity-free backup source of domestic heat is absolutely the way to go. For an additional level of comfort, you might consider a home-generated backup electricity source to supply at least partial central heating.

First, some central heating terminology. "Furnaces" refer to hot air systems and "boilers" mean hot water systems. Furnaces require large pumps to move air around. The running wattage for a furnace, including all electrical requirements, is approximately 1,400 to 1,680 watts (or 12 to 14 amps). However, many systems operate on less than 12 amps (1,400 watts). The starting wattage, which is only needed for one to one and a half seconds, is about 50 percent higher than the running wattage.

A boiler and its circulating pumps use less electricity—about 600 watts—to run the pumps, and about 900 watts to start. This is because much less power is required to move heated water through piping than to blow warm air through ducts. Oil burners consume 240 watts compared to a gas boiler, which draws 40 watts.

You can reduce the wattage requirement for a gas or oil boiler system by limiting the number of circulating pumps, which each draw approximately 130 watts. Pumps circulate water to specific sections of the home called "zones." Zones are designed to distinguish one area of the home from another, which allows you to choose different room temperatures in different zones. Homes can have one or several zones. The trick here is to reduce your living area—the number of zones you occupy—to conserve fuel and save wattage. If you have a gas system and heat one zone, it would only draw 680 watt-hours in four hours, while two zones would use 1,360 watt-hours. But these figures apply only if the pump runs continuously; in reality, it might run for as little as ten minutes out of each hour, depending on climatic considerations and the domestic heat load, using far fewer watts. It then becomes practical and relatively inexpensive to meet such a small electrical requirement with a renewable energy device, such solar electric cells or a small wind generator. But remember that, in addition to buying the components of the system you select, you will have to hire someone to wire the system safely.

DOMESTIC WATER SUPPLY

Most of us receive domestic water from a municipal system. We suggest that you write to your water district and ask them what steps they have taken to ensure compliance with Y2K corrections. You might also ask about any plans the water utility has for backup sources of electricity to ensure continued delivery of water (see chapter 7).

There are approximately 15 million wells in the U.S. and most of them will not work during an electrical outage because the device that pumps water to the house depends on electricity. Lack of water becomes unpleasant very quickly—you cannot cook, wash, flush the toilet, and there is no water to drink unless you have a supply of bottled water. This sounds dry even on paper, but you have to be there to experience the real discomfort.

If your water comes from a well, find out if you can use a manual pump. If a manual pump is not suitable, then a submersible pump fueled by a renewable energy source would be a good alternative. The least preferred alternative is a backup generator. However, for many people, a generator is the path of least resistance. We hope to convince you that the manual pump or the renewable energy alternative is safer and more prudent. If you have a sump pump in the basement, you need to install a manual pump to keep the basement dry during electrical outages.

Food Storage and Cooking

Refrigerators, freezers, electric ranges, and microwave ovens are the primary electricity-consuming appliances in the kitchen. Chapter 6 tells you how to create a domestic pantry, which is simply a long-term supply of nonperishable food that does not require refrigeration. This will change your customary food storage habits, but if a power outage makes your refrigerator and freezer useless, you can still have a reasonable supply of food stored in the pantry and/or a cool, dark root cellar. Combined with an electricity-free heating unit, which is capable of boiling water and cooking a limited amount of food, this system will be perfectly functional during the occasional or long-term electrical outage.

Home Lighting

Lighting is important, especially in the dark of winter, both for the ability to carry out your daily routines and for the psychological comfort light provides. It is no coincidence that light has come to symbolize life, hope, and truth, or that two major religions have festivals of light in December. Nor is it surprising that people often become disoriented and frightened in the dark.

It is important to determine your core lighting needs in the event that the power grid goes down for a week or even four weeks. In evaluating your lighting needs, think in terms of your basic requirements. Ask yourself these questions: Can you do the preliminary preparation for dinner during the day, using natural light? Can the children all do their homework in one room using a single lamp (presuming school is open)?

Do you read at night? What areas of the house and yard require light? Lights may be essential in the following areas:

- outside entryways or paths
- kitchen
- living or family room, where you tend to gather
- bedrooms
- bathroom
- stairways

There are many alternatives to utility-provided electric light. With a backup power source, you can continue to use your existing lighting system. In that case, we strongly recommend that you replace as many incandescent light bulbs as you can with longer lasting, more efficient fluorescent fixtures, particularly compact fluorescent light bulbs.

You do not need electricity to meet your lighting needs. The common standbys when the lights go out are candles, matches, and flashlights. You need an ample supply of candles—five days without power during the recent ice storm decimated our perceived large supply—and some sturdy candleholders. You also need plenty of spare batteries for flashlights. Every family member should have a flashlight. Candles should not be left burning after the family goes to sleep; an adult should be responsible for making sure all candles are out at night.

We have found through several emergencies that the romance of candles is short-lived. For a day or so, you can picture yourself as a second Abe Lincoln hitting the books by candlelight on the way to the presidency, or as an eighteenth-century heroine signaling your lover by candlelight, but it doesn't take more than twenty-four hours before you realize that candles provide just enough light to give you a headache after reading a few pages. Kerosene lamps are a better alternative, as they provide considerably more light. A few strategically placed kerosene lamps are an excellent source of backup lighting. Make sure you have plenty of kerosene to run them, and that it is stored safely outside the house out of the reach of children. Check with your municipal authorities about any rules governing kerosene storage in your location. And be certain an adult is at home to monitor the lamps because of the inherent risk of fire. Put the lamps out at night. Remember that the great Chicago fire of 1871 started when a cow kicked over a kerosene lamp in

O'Leary's barn. Check that your household fire alarm system is powered by an effective battery system, and is not dependent on the utility electric supply for its source of power.

SUNDRY ELECTRICAL NEEDS

Our homes are filled with devices requiring electricity that are unnecessary during the short-term inconvenience of an electrical outage. But one that is necessary is a functional radio. Many mail-order catalogs, including Gardener's Supply Company and Real Goods, carry a manual windup radio that can keep you in touch with the world. Particularly during a relatively long power outage, you will want to find out what is going on. Most of us can live without TVs, stereo systems, microwave ovens, dishwashers, toasters, washing machines and dryers, garage door openers, irons, and vacuum cleaners. These are conveniences, but life can function without them.

If you have a home office, or rely upon your home computer and printer for work, consider getting a portable computer and an ink jet printer, because their electrical requirements are far less than a desktop system and laser printer, and they can be powered by an affordable solar electrical system.

To repeat, electricity-free backup systems that are simple and reliable can fulfill essential home needs. Those who need or choose to generate a small amount of electricity can use effective and low-cost renewable energy systems, which, combined with good conservation practices, can keep your home quite comfortable. We ask you to consider solar and wind generation first. Standby fossil fuel-powered generators may be best for those who have special medical needs or are elderly or disabled.

Backup Power Options

Three basic methods can satisfy your critical home electric needs when the utility power grid goes down:

- a backup battery system combined with an inverter charged by utility power;
- a power generator fueled by fossil fuel or renewable energy;
- a combined generator/battery/inverter system.

Since we will be referring often to battery/inverter systems throughout the remainder of this chapter, let's explain how such a system works. In this system, batteries can be charged by utility power alone, and can be augmented by solar modules or a fossil-fueled generator as needed. Stored battery-power direct current (DC) is converted to alternating current (AC) as it passes through an inverter on route to satisfying the home's electrical needs. The duration of the charge depends upon battery size and quality as well as the draw-down rate. For more specific information, determine your critical electrical needs and the number of days you want reserve battery capacity, and choose a battery by the kilowatt-hours required to meet your estimated needs. Size the inverter to meet the peak watt requirement. Remember that the typical American house uses 10 to 15 kilowatt hours (kWh) per day.

The battery/inverter system is best for rolling blackouts because utility power recharges the batteries when it is available. It is also useful for power outages, the length of its usefulness being entirely dependent upon the size of the reserve and the demands placed upon the system.

One company, Real Goods (1-800-919-2400; www.realgoods.com), offers three battery/inverter kits ranging from $750 to $2,000. The least expensive one has a reserve of 2 kWh and the most costly one has a reserve of 8 kWh. The only way to operate such a system effectively is to use the power it provides to meet the lowest wattage and most important loads. Individual appliances must be connected to a separate electric distribution box that is connected to the inverter. The disadvantage of the battery/inverter system is that some batteries have only a three- to five-year life; even better-quality ones last just seven to ten years. Safety is a major consideration with conventional wet-cell batteries, because they release potentially explosive gases. This is the battery type with removable caps. If you store them in or near a house, place them in a sealed container vented to the outside. Sealed maintenance-free batteries are often a better choice for emergency power systems.

The most effective backup system combines a battery and inverter with small amounts of power generated on site, either from solar electric modules (also called photovoltaics), a wind plant, or a fossil-fuel-powered standby generator. We will discuss renewable energy systems first.

WATTAGE USE CHART

Household requirements	Running wattage requirements	Starting wattage requirements
Coffee maker		
brewing	1,200	0
warming	600	0
Dishwasher		
cool dry	700	1,400
hot dry	1,450	1,400
Electric fry pan	1,300	0
Electric range		
6" element	1,500	0
8" element	2,100	0
Microwave oven,		
625 watts	800	800
Refrigerator		
or freezer	700	2,200
Toaster		
2-slice	1,050	0
4-slice	1,650	0
Automatic washer		
vertical axis	650	1,500
horizontal axis	250	750
Clothes dryer		
gas	700	1,800
electric	5,750	1,800
Dehumidifier	650	800
Electric blanket	400	0
Garage door opener		
¼ horsepower	550	1,100
⅓ horsepower	725	1,400
Furnace fan, gas or fuel oil		
⅛ horsepower	300	500
⅙ horsepower	500	750
¼ horsepower	600	1,000
⅓ horsepower	700	1,400
½ horsepower	875	2,350
Hair dryer	300–1,200	0
Iron	1,200	0

Household requirements	Running wattage requirements	Starting wattage requirements
Lights	(as indicated on bulb)	
Radio	50–200	0
Well pump (submersible)		
⅓ horsepower	500	4,000
½ horsepower	1,000	5,500
Sump pump		
⅓ horsepower	800	1,300
½ horsepower	1,050	2,150
Television		
color (27")	200	0
black & white (19")	100	0
Vacuum Cleaner		
standard	800	0
deluxe	1,100	0
Central air conditioner		
10,000 BTU	1,500	2,200
20,000 BTU	2,500	3,300
24,000 BTU	3,800	4,950
32,000 BTU	5,000	6,500
40,000 BTU	6,000	7,800★
Computer		
laptop	45	0
CPU (usual)	40–50	0
(maximum)	155–200	0
monitor (15")	116	0
Printer		
laser	528–1,200	0
ink jet	14–35	0

★Courtesy of American Honda Motor Co., Inc., and Real Goods Trading Company, 1998.

Source: Independent Research: Karen Moore

This technical information is given as an example; for specific information on individual products, contact manufacturers or the equipment supplier.

Providing Backup Electricity with Renewables: Solar and Wind

Dermot has spent much of his life working in the renewable energy field and he is enthusiastic about the use of renewable energy systems. Solar and wind electric systems deserve consideration, both for routine use, and as excellent emergency backup. While some domestic solar electric and wind electric systems are still complex and costly, relatively inexpensive renewable energy systems are available that can meet small electrical loads, such as a few lights, a low-wattage computer, one pump in a hot water heating system, or even a submersible pump. An easy place to start if you have an interest in solar energy is a solar-powered portable energy system. These systems are designed to deliver 3 to 18 volts of electricity at 9.9 watts. They deliver enough charging power to run a laptop computer, radio, or cell phone. They are small enough to be tucked under your arm and can be propped up virtually anywhere to soak in the sun's energy.

Forget for a moment all of the electric gizmos and gadgets in the typical home, and instead focus on powering one or two or perhaps three electric devices that would be useful to have function even in an emergency. The key to lower-cost, technology-simple, renewable energy electric supply is delivering it to a small or even a micro electricity load. The basic components of such a delivery system include a small array of solar electric modules (each 2 feet by 4 feet) or a small wind generator, a small battery bank (two golf cart batteries), and an inverter. A system like this could generate enough electricity to power your laptop computer, some lights, or even, as the following example demonstrates, the minimal operation of your central heating system during an emergency.

Many homes in America are heated by a natural gas or propane boiler supplying a hot water-based heating system separated into multiple zones. Let us assume that you have a gas boiler that draws 40 watts when it is fired and each zone has a circulating pump drawing 130 watts. By restricting the heating system to a single zone, you could enjoy heat in one section of the house, for a total of 170 watts. If the pump and boiler operate on average for about ten minutes an hour, that would use a total of 360 watt-hours for up to twelve hours of useful or at least background heat in any given day. If the boiler were to fire for 15 minutes every hour, you would have eight hours of boiler operation for the same daily consumption of 360 watt-hours.

Two or three 75-watt solar electric modules provide an average of 350 watt-hours per day in many parts of the U.S. Even in some of the darker, northern climates, such as Vermont, three 75-watt panels may provide 320 watt-hours per day on average, after deducting 30 percent for battery, inverter, and other losses. Vermont receives average sunlight of about two hours per day in the worst month of the year. (The Solarex Corporation has created a detailed map of solarization, which is reproduced in *The Solar Living Sourcebook*. This information is available in table form in *The Passive Solar House* by James Kachadorian. See the bibliography.) A sunnier climate, which includes most of the rest of America, can produce a small but useful supply of renewable electricity from two modules in really sunny locations. A two-panel system including the panels, inverter, charge controller, volt meter, and two golf cart batteries starts at about $1,800 (plus installation).

If your gas boiler is hard-wired into a 220-amp system, you will need an additional transformer to take the voltage from the inverter level of 120 volts to 220 volts, and that costs about $350. You will also need the services of an electrician. Many new boilers and heat zone pumps are simply plugged into an electrical socket. An extension cord running from the inverter can be used to supply these needs, and as such there is no need to disconnect from the electrical utility by using a transfer switch, because there is no danger of backfeeding into the utility (see below).

As another example, let's say that the need that is important for you to meet is a well pump and let's assume you have a 1/3-horsepower (HP) pump that consumes a running wattage of 750 watts. A photovoltaic system generating 360 watt-hours of electricity per day will operate your water pump for one-half hour in a twenty-four-hour day. For purposes of emergency backup, the homeowner has a real need for as little as two gallons of water per person per day. The average domestic well pump need operate for a very short period of time in order to satisfy this demand, which means that other small household electrical loads could be met, such as a few efficient, compact fluorescent lights. Sump and submersible pumps draw a significant starting wattage for a fraction of a second. To meet such needs, four golf-cart-type batteries are better than two.

The solar electric module/battery/inverter system suggested here will provide three or more days' supply of a very small electrical load. However, in some regions of the U.S., two weeks of constant cloud coverage in the dark of winter can easily occur once or twice a season. Talk with your solar electric module provider or a renewable energy consultant about the likelihood of gaining even a small amount of usable current on cloudy or diffuse sunlight days in your particular area. Climatic conditions can limit the functional usefulness of solar modules even for backup situations.

This brings us to small wind power machines for meeting micro or small electricity loads. To meet any appreciable percentage of the electric needs of the typical American home with a wind generator is out of the question for many reasons, not least of which is zoning. A wind generator rotates at high speed and creates a low background sound that some people find annoying. It must be located 20 or 30 feet above any obstruction within at least a 200-foot radius, preferably a 500-foot radius. To install a wind generator that would come even close to creating the electric output provided by a standby generator would cost anywhere from $8,000 to $16,000, and would require a much greater level of attention, maintenance, and care.

On the other hand, a very small wind power system producing 25 to 100 watts in a 15 mph or greater wind can cost as little as $1,200 to $2,000, including a basic battery and inverter pack. This is about the same price as a fossil fuel-powered generator or a small photovoltaic system, and may be useful for small electrical loads, if the balance of your home has simple electricity-free backup systems.

Like a small array of solar modules, a small wind generation system can partially supply your domestic electrical loads year-round, and it can serve as a useful source of backup electricity in an emergency. If your home is located in a windmill-friendly environment, you can replace the suggested two or three 75-watt solar electric modules with a single wind generator.

Many makes of wind generators are available in the marketplace today; all of them have redeeming qualities, and all of them have unique features. For the low-budget micro or small size, a useful recommendation is the Southwest Wind Power Air 403, a recent replacement of the model 303. The Air 403 is rated at a peak 400 watts in a wind speed of about 30 miles an hour. This small, three-bladed wind generator is fairly quiet, with a simple rugged design. It retails for about $600 and has a charge controller built into it, which stops the generator from over-charging batteries. A tower will cost about $400. The balance of the components, basic battery, and inverter pack remain the same, bringing the total cost for a basic system to about $1,800, the same as a two-module solar electric system. Get expert feedback on the site where you intend to locate the wind generator, and by all means ensure that your neighbors will not object to this small, unobtrusive machine. All wind generators create a sound that is different from the sound of background wind, no matter how small and quiet they are. Wind machines are obviously better suited to rural or sparsely populated areas and not to dense suburban areas.

A word about batteries. First, determine your electricity requirements. For example, if you want to run four 25-watt light fixtures for three hours per day, the daily load will equal 300 watt-hours. Two typical golf cart batteries are rated at 220 amps at 12 volts. To calculate the watt-hours stored, multiply amps by volts, which equals 2,640 watt-hours. For emergency use, batteries should not be drawn down by more than 80 percent of the peak charge, so one golf cart battery will yield a functional 2,000 watt-hours of storage. This in turn will allow a 300 watt-hour per day draw-down for a six-day period. To determine the battery needs of your system, multiply the daily watt-hour requirement by the number of days you would like the storage to last, and factor in an 80 percent draw-down.

One advantage of a small renewable electric system is that the inverter allows the batteries to be maintained at peak charge level by the electric utility when electricity is available from the grid. The homeowner needs to be careful about the choice of inverter. We recommend a transformer-based inverter. Transformer-based inverters come with a battery charger. They are also capable of handling the higher starting wattage requirements. Pumps often require five to eight times the running wattage to get them pumping, and this starting wattage draw lasts for no more than a fraction of a second. Less expensive electronic switching inverters are starting to flood the market. These are not capable of handling startup surges and they will not recharge the battery from the utility grid.

Another benefit of renewable energy electricity even for emergency use is that the simple system is probably more reliable than a standby fossil fuel-powered electric generator, and the homeowner need not continually find a source of fuel supply, particularly gasoline. If you are concerned about lengthy regional power outages due to Y2K, take note that the gas stations will be as incapable of operating as the electric utility, so the source of generator fuel will not be available. More importantly, for those who have the resources to purchase renewable electric power, the systems are environmentally friendly and quiet, they introduce the homeowner to the practicality of renewable energy in a relatively low-cost way, and they allow for future expansion of the system either as prices for the technology continue to come down, or if, as the result of fortuitous circumstances, one's discretionary budget increases.

Remember that solar- or wind-generated electricity is most effective for meeting small and micro electric loads, including some home boiler needs, water pump needs, and essential home office needs for portable computers and ink jet printers. Loading more household electrical appliances onto compact, relatively low-cost renewable energy systems dramatically increases their cost. For example, oil-fired hot air furnaces and blowers consume 1,000 to 1,600 watts when operating. If an oil furnace system drawing a running wattage of 1,400 watts were used during a power outage for just ten minutes out of every hour over a twelve-hour period, it would consume 2,800 watt-hours, a multiple of almost eight times what the gas-fired, single-zone hot water heating system would consume. Weather permitting, the latter can supply at least one heat zone using only two solar modules costing $1,000; for the oil hot air system, you would need as many as sixteen modules costing $8,000, plus the expense of a bigger battery and inverter system. Today's solar module prices are about $5 per watt, and it wasn't so long ago that they were closer to $100 per watt, so we may continue to see a dramatic decrease in price.

Providing Backup Electricity with a Fossil Fuel-powered Generator

The alternative to backup electricity generated by renewable energy sources is a fossil fuel-powered backup generator. Generators are noisy and can release smelly fumes into the air. Generators depend on a supply of a combustible fuel and require utility protection devices, which can be expensive. However, despite their disadvantages, generators appeal to many people as a quick fix for emergency backup power.

As we said above, it is preferable to meet all your core needs without electricity. However, if you still want or need home-generated electricity, plan to limit its use to essentials. For example, you may be able to heat and cook with a woodstove, and save the electricity for other needs. Give some thought to the efficiency of your lights, refrigerator, and other appliances. If it is time to upgrade them, consider buying electricity-free appliances, such as a propane stove. You will save on your electric bills and need less backup power during an emergency.

The purpose of reducing needs is to be able to design an emergency power system that is practical from a technology, wiring, and cost perspective. Some large contemporary homes would need a generator as big as the Ritz to function normally. That is not a practical approach for most people because of the cost and the fact that the majority of emergencies last for a limited period of time.

During a power outage, many people buy the nearest generator that they can find, which is most often portable and gasoline powered. This may not be the best choice for your family's needs. Many generators are not designed for continual use, and some may burn out if run continuously for as few as three days. Since you are planning ahead, you can take the time to consider safety, size, quality, speed, noise, and fuel requirements of home generators. Careful choice will give you greater service.

DURABILITY, NOISE, AND MAINTENANCE

In assessing your generator needs, first pay attention to the run time of the generator. Run time refers to how long the generator can operate continuously without stressing the engine. Some generators are designed only for light duty and occasional use, and are likely to break down if asked to run continuously. Second, if you want to avoid being outcast by your neighbors, make sure the generator you buy is designed to run quietly. No one wants the irritation of a small engine making a big noise within a few feet of their home for hours on end. The noise level is related to the revolutions per minute (rpm) and the quality of construction. Third, determine how long the generator will run on one tankful (operational capacity). The sales literature, owner's manual, and your local dealer can help you make the best choice for your needs.

Variable loads stress a generator and use fuel inefficiently. A variable electrical load can occur, for example, when your furnace fan kicks on and off. Your furnace fan only requires electricity when it is called upon to distribute heat throughout your home. To have a generator operating continuously in order to meet minimum electrical needs, such as lighting, and then force it to kick in with heavy horsepower use for the furnace fan or boiler pump, imposes a variable load on the generator.

A useful idea is to combine your gas generator system with a battery/inverter. This will allow you to run your generator at peak efficiency for shorter periods of time, charging the batteries, which will then provide a reservoir of energy that the inverter will convert to household current. When a generator is operated for an extended period to meet a small load, it operates inefficiently and tends to clog up. The battery/inverter system will meet your electric needs quietly, so you and your neighbors can enjoy a night's rest.

Maintenance measures include keeping the generator cool and supplied with fresh air while in operation, and, if it is not a continuous-use generator, operating it only as long as the manufacturer recommends before letting it cool down and rest. It is important to start the generator periodically and let it run for an hour or so as an additional maintenance measure. Do not store gasoline in a generator. Ask your dealer about periodic checks and tune-ups.

SAFETY FIRST

This chapter is not intended to replace your electrician. It merely points out things to consider when purchasing a generator system, but you should discuss the details with a qualified electrician. If you do purchase a system on your own, you should have an electrician install the equipment. An improperly installed generator feeds power back into the utility grid and could shock or kill linemen working near your home. Or it can feed electricity into a neighbor's home, causing damage to their electrical equipment. If the power comes back on while your generator is operating, it can damage the generator, other electrical appliances in your home, and even cause a fire. Unless you are an electrician, do not install a backup generator yourself.

An electrician can install a device called a transfer switch to safely integrate your generator with your existing panel. The automatic transfer switch isolates the generator from the utility line at all times and prevents utility power from feeding into your generator, or vice versa, causing damage or injury. A transfer switch and installation can cost between $500 and $700, depending on the wattage and/or amperage of the switch. When utility power comes on after an outage, the transfer switch automatically reconnects the domestic load with utility service. Transfer switches come in different shapes and sizes with different features. Some automatically switch your entire household electric circuit to the generator and others call for selective manual switching among chosen appliances. By working with an electrician now, you can be ready for any power outages that may occur.

Another safety consideration is the location of the power generator. Don't install it inside your home or garage. Generators must have proper and adequate ventilation. There is no point in having heat and light only to expire from fumes. Some generators are manufactured to be outdoors at all times; they come in a protective metal case and are quite happy in virtually any weather. Others may need some protection. Consult the manual that comes with the generator and ask an electrician about correct placement.

You should ground the generator to prevent electric shock. You can purchase a grounding rod from any hardware store. They are typically 8 feet long and $5/8$ inch in diameter, with a copper-clad exterior and iron interior. The grounding rod is driven into the ground, and connected to the generator with a copper wire. Fuel storage is another safety issue. See the section on fuel storage later in this chapter.

WHAT SIZE GENERATOR DO YOU NEED?

You should consult an electrician about the optimum-size generator for your home, but we suggest that you start by considering a 3,500-watt to 5,000-watt generator rated at 30 amps and producing 240/120 volts. These are fairly common sizes for standby generators and one can probably satisfy your home's most basic needs, including well pump, refrigerator, lights, furnace fan and ignition, radio, and, perhaps, some appliances. They will probably not power your electric hot water heater or electric range, but will supply your core needs. You may need to switch some appliances on and off manually to avoid overloading the generator, particularly the 3,500-watt size. Generators should not be operated at their maximum power output for more than thirty minutes at a time. A generator equipped with a single port, as opposed to multiple ports, may be easier to install.

A 6,500-watt generator will allow you to use air-conditioning under some circumstances. Read the chapter on cooling for alternative ideas before consulting with an electrician. If you want to be able to use your electric water heater and electric range, which usually require 240 volts, in addition to the basic needs mentioned above, you will need a 7,500-watt generator. Do not plan to use an electric generator to provide electric space heating, as it is a waste of fuel and will cause excessive wear and tear.

Rated power is a better gauge of generator power than maximum power. Rated power is the power a generator can produce for extended periods of time. Be careful when you shop; generators are marketed by their maximum power, not their rated power. For example, if you buy a 5,000-watt generator, the rated power is only 4,500 watts. As a rough gauge, rated power is generally 90 percent of the maximum power. Consider your needs in relation to the rated wattage of the generator you choose.

TYPE OF GENERATOR AND FUEL STORAGE

If you choose to buy a fossil fuel-powered generator, you need to consider fuel storage and safety issues. There are four different types of generator fuels: gasoline, propane, natural gas, and diesel. While most generators purchased in an emergency are gasoline generators, they may not be best. A multi-fuel generator, one that can burn two or three fuels—propane, natural gas, or gasoline—is a good choice. Propane adapter kits can be purchased for some makes of gasoline generators, and these would qualify as multi-fuel generators. Diesel generators can burn only diesel fuel, and tend to represent a very limited portion of the market for backup generators.

Analyze your personal needs and desired comfort level before you decide on the amount of fuel to store. Obviously, the more fuel you have in times of need, the more your neighbors will visit. The first step is to determine your core electrical needs—those items you cannot live without. Determine the amperage and voltage of those items and then multiply amps by volts to get the required wattage. It may be as simple as reading a label attached to an appliance motor, or referring to an owner's manual. The chart on pages 34–35 gives wattage requirements for many items found in the typical home. You can also visit Honda's Web site at www.honda.com and use their household watt calculator to determine the total wattage of your core electrical needs.

Once you have this information, you can determine the appropriate size generator and the amount of fuel you need to store. Remember— the larger the generator, the higher the fuel consumption.

Gasoline

The weakness inherent in gasoline generators is the fuel. Be aware that there is a "use date" for gasoline storage because the quality of gasoline degrades in as little as three months. The duration of gasoline storage is related to the octane level of the fuel; higher-octane gasoline can be stored longer. Rotate your gasoline every three months and use the older gasoline in your car.

Manufacturers recommend that gasoline generators be stored with an empty gas tank. You do not want your generator filled with degraded gas when you most need it, as it may not work. Avoid the temptation of keeping the generator tank full as a way of adding to your fuel reserve.

It is a violation of federal law to store gas in a container that is not designated a fuel storage container. These containers clearly indicate their contents and have a vented cap. Needless to say, gasoline is extremely flammable, so do not under any circumstances store it in your house. Because gasoline vapors are denser than air, they can collect in poorly vented areas.

Auxiliary fuel tanks added directly to gasoline generators can create additional pressure on the inlet needle valve, which can cause it to improperly regulate fuel flowing into the carburetor. When this happens, it can damage the engine and cause fuel leaks. Read your manual carefully before installation, and follow the manufacturer's guidelines.

Each state has reporting guidelines for spills. In New York, for example, you must report spills of over two gallons and failure to report can result in a fine. If a spill causes gasoline to soak into the ground, cleanup can be both difficult and expensive. Spilled gas can travel distances and affect groundwater and well water.

Having an adequate store of gasoline for your backup generator is a concern. Gas generators use about one gallon of gas per hour. Many people assume that the 20-gallon tank or reserve tucked away in the garage would be adequate for any power outage. Actually, a 20-gallon reserve is adequate for about a day. Effective use of limited gas reserve can be greatly extended by using a battery/inverter system and moderating the electric load. When calculating your storage needs, remember that the northeastern ice storm of January 1998 left over 3 million people without power for days, and some for six weeks, and the southeastern ice storm in December 1998 left tens of thousands without power and heat for a week.

The idea when preparing for an emergency is to have an ample or an adequate reserve of fuel, which means more fuel rather than less. However, with gasoline, there is an inherent conflict: the more gasoline you have, the more attention you must pay to care, planning, storage, and rotation. Gasoline use calls for extreme caution, both for the environment and your personal safety.

Propane

A propane generator is a good choice for the homeowner who heats with propane or oil. Propane can be safely stored at your home and the tank can be buried in the ground without danger to the environment. If it spills, the ground will temporarily freeze and then thaw with no permanent damage incurred. It is flammable, however, so use caution and follow safety measures as you would with any fuel.

If you already heat with propane, you can draw on your fuel reserves. Keep fuel deliveries frequent and your tank topped off. You may want to increase your overall storage capacity. Many propane dealers will supply a free storage tank when you sign a fuel supply agreement. Storage tanks come in a variety of sizes: 24, 50, 100, 120, 250, 330, or 500 gallons, while 1,000-gallon storage tanks are often available for a fee. Sometimes a supplier will offer a 1,000-gallon tank at no cost if the estimated fuel consumption warrants it. For those of you who heat with oil, but will be using a propane backup generator, a 120-gallon propane tank may be a good place to start.

Your supplier can arrange a permanent hookup from the tank to the propane generator, barbecue grill, cook top, or any other propane appliance you choose. You could have an RV-style propane refrigerator as a backup. Be sure these appliances are properly vented.

If you buy a gasoline-fired generator, consider purchasing a model that has an optional propane gas adapter. Then you can install a propane tank at your home, and have an electrician set up your system so that it functions using either gasoline or propane.

Natural Gas

If you heat with natural gas, a natural gas-fired backup generator is an option. Utility-supplied natural gas is definitely vulnerable to the effects of Y2K, but probably not to the extent that electric utilities are. To quote one gas utility representative, "the natural gas system is salted with embedded chips, many of them for safety reasons." Thus it is not the most resilient fuel for a backup generator. Moreover, you have zero storage capability with natural gas. Although earthquakes can obviously interfere with natural gas delivery, this fuel is relatively immune to severe weather. If you favor natural gas, consider buying a multi-fuel generator that can burn propane, gasoline, or natural gas. Even with natural gas, you might want to consider adding a battery/inverter system, depending on the run-time of the generator and its ability to handle variable loads.

Diesel

Diesel generators are another option. Diesel is a heavier oil than gasoline and less combustible. It stores well without degeneration over time. A diesel generator would be a deluxe model of fossil fuel-based resilience for you to consider if you have a diesel automobile or truck, a diesel-fuel storage tank and generator, plus a backup battery/inverter.

GENERATOR COSTS

Although you can purchase a fossil-fuel generator for as little as $400 to $600, we don't recommend the cheaper models. Prices vary due to many factors, including size, engine make, features, and durability. We suggest an opening price point of $1,000 for a single-fuel model to get the quality and reliability in a generator that is important. Depending on the size, you may pay $1,600 or more for a respectable bi-fuel generator, and up to $4,000 for a larger tri-fuel generator unit of 8,000 watts. Honda is introducing the EUX, a new, lightweight, 3,000-watt generator that uses gasoline for fuel and has a computer-controlled sine-wave inverter, which enables precise control of frequency and tension variations, making it an excellent source of power for high-precision electronic equipment, including computers. Because it does not have any embedded microprocessors, it is Y2K-compliant. According to the company, the price will compare to regular generators.

By taking the time now to choose the best generating system for your family's needs, and by storing a comfortable level of fuel, you will avoid last-minute scrambles and costly mistakes during a power outage. You can then feel very comfortable, knowing you have taken the steps necessary to preserve the comfort and enjoyment of your home.

CHAPTER 3

HEATING WITH WOOD AND OTHER
FORMS OF RENEWABLE ENERGY

I'll be laying in some extra wood [before December 31, 1999].

VERMONT SENATOR PATRICK LEAHY,
News Conference, December 29, 1998

 THE CENTRAL HEATING SYSTEM of the average American home is highly vulnerable to Y2K and other mishaps. If the power goes out, your central heating system probably will not work, since electricity is necessary for fans, pumps, ignition, thermostat, and other control functions. Fuel supplies may be delayed, and prices may spike because of unforeseen international conditions. Add to that the complex technology of your furnace, and the difficulty getting hold of a repairman if your furnace should break down in the middle of the night, and you may be ready to consider a heating system that uses locally available, renewable energy sources such as wood and solar energy.

This chapter begins with tips on insulation and solar gain, since these measures can benefit any home, no matter what type of heating system is used. Next, we discuss the merits of heating with wood, talk about recent improvements in the design of wood stoves, and relate the pros and cons of stoves, fireplace inserts, and more. Finally, we touch upon the use of solar, wind, and water energy as heating fuels. As will become apparent, our preference is for the use of renewable energy: wood where the Sun is shy, and solar, or a combination of wood and solar, in sunny regions.

Tightening the Envelope

There is no getting around the fact that the topic of insulation is, to most of us, a deeply boring subject. Even so, we urge you to overcome any resistance to conducting an energy audit of your house; weatherization can make a big difference to the comfort of your home. Not only that, but a well-insulated home will help conserve natural resources, since it will require less energy to heat.

In an emergency, where your source of heat is limited, good insulation could make the difference between staying in or leaving your home. A house loses its heat in direct relationship to the quality of its insulation. A well-insulated, tight home will retain its residual warmth much longer than a poorly insulated, drafty one, and will benefit disproportionately from any heat input, even from the presence of active people and pets, who all emit a useful amount of thermal energy. A well-insulated home gives you the option, in an emergency, of heating only one or two rooms, and closing off the rest. This becomes a more challenging exercise in the poorly insulated house, because if you retreat to a smaller area, there is the chance that water pipes lying outside the heated rooms may freeze. Clearly the well-insulated home will retain peripheral heat for a longer period, and will require less heat input to maintain it above the critical freezing point.

In a condition of real emergency, where you choose to leave your home, or close off parts of the house, be sure to drain the water from any of the pipes that might freeze, and add antifreeze solution to areas that can't be easily drained, such as toilet bowls, and sink elbows. However, if you do the things recommended in this book, its unlikely that you will ever need to take such a radical step.

One caveat about tight houses: Remember that if you do any renovating, such as installing new carpet, painting, or adding new furniture, these items often contain toxic fumes that need to be aired out of your house. For those of you who plan to struggle along with an open fireplace as backup heat during a power outage, remember that an open fireplace needs an intake of air to work; you will need to keep a window partially open. Also, recent reports suggest that a too-tightly closed-up home can lead to increased colds in the wintertime.

Even with these precautions in mind, chances are your home could do with extra insulation. Start by noting any drafty areas. Check the weatherstripping around doors, and the caulking around window panes and electrical outlets. Check for cracks in the foundation and exterior walls and other areas where outside air could be entering the house.

If you turn down the heat, how quickly do different parts of the house lose their warmth? What are the obvious ways the heat escapes; for example, through north-facing windows, or poorly weatherstripped kitchen doors? How does the R-value of the insulation in the walls and the attic compare with the recommendations provided by the U.S. Department of Energy? (See sidebar.) Do your windows have double panes? Do you have insulated drapes or quilts to draw over the windows at night? Be aggressive with your review. Imagine the optimum situation for your house and compare it to the actual status of your home.

Unless you have a brand-new house, your review of the state of the insulation is bound to show some weak areas. Obviously, you should fix them by adding insulation where needed in the walls and attic. If you plan to replace your home's windows, get the best-insulated windows that you can, because cold windows draw heat away from people near them. Heat from the warm human body radiates to cold surfaces; a well-insulated window will increase your personal level of comfort.

Insulation

Since warm air rises, the best place to add insulation is in the attic. This will help keep your upper floors warm. Recommended insulation levels depend on where you live and the type of heating system you use. For most climates a minimum of R-30 will do, but colder areas, such as North Dakota, Minnesota, Northern Maine, and Vermont, and the parts of Montana, Wyoming, and Colorado that abut the Rocky Mountains may need as much as R-49. As a rule of thumb, the Department of Energy (DOE) says most homes in the U.S. should have between R-19 and R-49 insulation in the attic. Two useful booklets, DOE/CE-0180 (dated August 1997), and DOE/GO-10097-431 (dated September 1997), provide information about insulating materials and insulation levels needed in various locations by zip code. You can obtain them by writing to the U.S. Department of Energy, Office of Technical Information,

In addition, it is a good idea to contact your electric utility and ask if they conduct energy audits for customers. Many utilities, including natural gas utilities, provide this useful and effective service, often through third-party providers, who serve as consultants only and do not get involved in selling or installing materials. In many states, utilities must provide their customers with mandated energy-efficiency programs. These efforts may be patterned on a voluntary national program administered by the Environmental Protection Agency (EPA), called the Energy Star Program (www.energystar.gov/).

The purpose of the Energy Star Program is to provide resources for more efficient use of energy in the home. Programs vary by state and by utility. "Star," "Energy Star," "Energy-Rated Homes," "Good Sense," and "Energy Crafted Homes" are some of the names for these organizations, which are generally non-profit. For the most part, they are staffed by knowledgeable people, who will help you identify the weaknesses in your home insulation, and those areas in your home where energy use can be improved by more efficient appliances.

One device that all these organizations have, or should have, is a blower door. This powerful extractor fan is placed inside the frame of a storm door and creates negative pressure inside the house, which pulls air through all the weak or missing insulation spots that visual inspection might miss.

In addition, these organizations will help you identify the

PO Box 62, Oak Ridge, TN 37831; calling them at 423-576-2286 or 576-8401; or visiting their Web sites at http://www.ornl.gov/roofs+walls or http://www.eren.doe.gov.

There are four types of insulating materials: batts, rolls, loose-fill, and rigid foam boards. Each is suitable for various parts of your house. Batts, designed to fit between the studs in the walls and the joists in the ceilings, are usually made of fiberglass or rock wool. Fiberglass combines sand and recycled glass; rock wool comes from basaltic rock mixed with materials that are recycled from the wastes of steel mills. Rolls are also made of fiberglass and can be laid on the attic floor. Contractors blow loose-fill insulation, which is made of fiberglass, rock wool, or cellulose, into attics and walls. Rigid board insulation, designed for confined spaces such as basements, foundations, and exterior walls, provides additional structural support. It is also suitable for cathedral ceilings best way to get the job done, and will often recommend material and installers. If, because of their non-profit status, third-party organizations are not free to recommend contractors, talk to your electric utility again and ask for recommendations. It is worthwhile to research this area thoroughly so you find topnotch contractors and are charged a fair price for work of good quality.

Passive Solar Gain

Once your home has been thoroughly insulated and tightened, you can turn your attention to passive solar gain. Anyone who has relaxed on a glassed-in porch on a cool autumn day knows how the Sun's rays can warm the interior. Most homes receive direct sunlight for at least part of the day. As the Earth turns, and the Sun appears to travel across the sky, it sends warming rays through the windows facing east, south, and west, in that order. North-facing windows do not receive direct sun. Even in the winter, the Sun's rays can make a significant contribution to the warmth of your house.

The key to passive solar gain is to allow the maximum available sunlight in during the day, and, as that sunlight fades away, to use insulated window quilts or another effective means of sealing in the warmth. In most climates, you also will need an additional heat source to keep your house warm. Even so, this passive solar gain can reduce your need to burn fuel; in an emergency, a home that makes good use of passive solar gain will stay warmer than a home that does not.

The Sun brings warmth and light into your home at no extra cost. Partially clear away shrubbery and dense trees to let the winter sunshine into your home, while keeping enough landscape cover to shade your home from the heat of the summer sun. For longer-term planning, you can plant deciduous trees, which will shade your windows in the summer and then drop their leaves in the winter. You can also retrofit your house by installing a concrete floor in a room that receives maximum sun. The concrete will absorb the heat from the Sun during the day and radiate it into the home in the evening. Concrete floors that have been colored and polished can be a decorative element in your home.

Y2K reminds us to pay attention to conserving energy, to reduce the burden on an already stressed infrastructure. Something as simple as turning down thermostats at night can make a big difference, if enough people do it. In any event, optimizing passive solar gain, and attending to the insulation of your home, form a solid basis from which to plan a resilient home heating system.

Wood Stoves

An efficient wood stove (or fireplace insert) could become an important part of your life, thanks to Y2K. But even without Y2K, the arguments for heating with wood are compelling:

Wood stoves do not require electricity. Because they operate without it, they are a resilient form of heat, not subject to the vagaries of stormy weather or Y2K. You can heat water and cook food on most models, which is useful when your electric range or microwave do not work.

Wood stoves bring peace of mind. There is great comfort in knowing, as the darkening days of November arrive, that your home has a good and efficient stove, and that your yard is stocked with one or more cords of seasoned wood.

Wood is a locally available resource, and easily stored. Given Y2K, there is no guarantee that oil, gas, and electric companies will continue to supply their products without interruption. With wood, you can plan ahead; a call to your local wood supplier will provide you with all the fuel you need for the winter. (Of course, firewood is not readily available everywhere, and heating with wood may not be the best option in some areas.)

Wood is a form of renewable energy. Fossil fuels are being consumed at an alarming rate. As wood is harvested, new trees can be planted, thus providing an endless supply of heating fuel. In areas of dense population and heavy wood use, special efforts must be made to sustainably harvest and replenish the forests.

Wood stoves are environmentally friendly. Burning fossil fuels releases carbon dioxide into the air, which contributes to the greenhouse effect and global climate change. Burning wood also releases carbon dioxide, but improved designs in wood stoves now keep these emissions to a minimum (see below). And as newly planted trees grow, they absorb carbon dioxide, thus maintaining a balance in the environment.

Overcoming a Bad Reputation

During and after the Arab oil embargo of the 1970s, over a thousand stove manufacturing companies rushed into the market, and that led to the installation of millions of stoves with high emission levels. This pollution caused trouble, particularly in western states. In some states, frequently at higher elevations, emissions became a significant and visible pollution problem. This left a regrettable legacy—the false impression that all wood stoves are environmentally unsound. Nothing could be further from the truth, at least for stoves built within the last few years. Sadly, more than 90 percent of existing wood stoves are based on old and inefficient technology and really should be replaced.

About a decade ago, the Environmental Protection Agency instigated a wood stove certification process, and all wood stoves sold today must be compliant with EPA regulations. The result is that high-efficiency wood stoves are now available. The first real breakthrough came with the addition of catalytic converters to stoves, which greatly reduced stovepipe emissions and increased efficiency. Since the introduction of catalytic converters, wood stove design has evolved to the point where today, for practical purposes, the benefits of pollution reduction and efficiency gain achieved by catalytic converters are equaled by creative techniques in firebox design, which result in the secondary combustion of gases.

New improved designs have made wood stoves the heating method of choice for many people. New models operate with up to 70 percent efficiency, minimizing pollution and consuming less fuel. (Many existing oil furnaces operate at lower efficiencies than newer wood stoves.) As an added advantage, you will not need to store and haul logs to your stove at anything like the rate that was necessary with an older, less efficient stove. Bev found that she could keep her seven-room home warm during the power outage caused by the 1998 ice storm by running two wood stoves, one in her living room, and one in the downstairs master bedroom, simply because warm air rose and kept the three rooms upstairs quite comfortable. You can begin by using a wood stove as backup for your central heating system. Then, having experienced the benefits of heating with wood, perhaps you will be motivated to use your stove as a primary source of heat for everyday use.

IF YOU HAVE AN OLD STOVE

You may have an older model stove, possibly one you have not used in some time. Your first step should be to determine its efficiency, and whether it meets EPA standards. Check with your wood stove dealer, or the manufacturer if they are still in business; many manufacturers are not. Unless it has a catalytic converter, chances are it does not meet EPA standards, and you would not want to use this stove on a regular basis. However, it may be useful as an emergency backup, until you are able to purchase a newer model.

If you have an existing stove with a catalytic converter, pay attention to cleaning the converter and replacing it on a routine basis, otherwise the efficiency of your stove will decrease and the pollution it produces will increase. Check the door seal for leaks. If you haven't used the stove in some time, we recommend that you call the chimney sweep and have your chimney cleaned. At the same time, you can ask the sweep's opinion of the condition of your stove, pipe, and chimney. You can then choose whether to keep your existing stove and lay in a cord or two of wood, or to purchase a new, high-efficiency model. The obvious benefits of buying a new stove include efficiency, less pollution, and the need for much less wood.

HOW TO CHOOSE A NEW STOVE

Before visiting your local stove shop, determine the square foot area of the space you need to heat. Better yet, draw a simple diagram of your home, and the rooms you want to heat, including the length, width, and ceiling height of each room. Be sure to tell the salesperson the status of your home's insulation. With this information, the salesperson will be able to help you choose a stove best suited to your needs.

Don't be surprised to receive a recommendation for a smaller stove than you would have chosen. With the new improved designs, even a small stove can generate a great deal of heat; some of the smallest will heat up to 800 square feet. Ask for advice on the placement of the stove.

Since most stoves provide radiant heat, they are best situated in open spaces within the home. Avoid locating a stove in a small room or a cramped space. Stoves that are too big for the space or the house in which they are located are a common problem. This almost always leads to a poorly operating stove.

The salesperson may try to steer you toward a gas-fired appliance; the majority of sales of what are now called hearth appliances (instead of stoves) burn gas rather than wood. They come equipped with artificial logs and look like stoves or fireplaces; some of them even have remote-control buttons. A wood stove has many advantages over these gas-burning appliances. Wood is a renewable energy resource and locally available, while gas is not. The next chapter discusses the pros and cons of gas-burning stoves.

At the stove shop, you will see models that have a catalytic converter, and others that do not. Compare efficiencies, because some of the newer models without catalytic converters are equal to those with them. Bear in mind that you must replace the catalytic converter about every four years in a steadily used wood stove, at a cost of about $160. Also at issue are the materials that go into manufacturing the catalyst, which later becomes trash; there is a net benefit if that waste can be avoided while efficiency is maintained.

While most stoves heat radiantly, many of them combine both radiant and convective heating, and some models provide predominantly convective heat. Convective wood stoves are fireboxes within a metal shroud or casing, which conduct heat via air circulation. In our opinion, radiant heat bestows a warming capacity to the human frame that hot-air systems can never approach. However, a radiant stove needs to be located in a large area. A convective wood stove, or combination of convective and radiant technology, may be the better choice in some circumstances; ask your dealer about your particular situation. Many stoves have protective metal sheeting at the rear. This promotes a small amount of convective heating, but the heat predominantly radiates out into the room.

The cost of a new stove system, including the stove pad, wall protection, and chimney installation, starts at about $1,500 to $1,900 for an installed, clean-burning stove. The cost of the wood stove itself ranges from a low of $600 to as much as $2,000. A larger, top-of-the-line stove plus installation can easily run $2,500 or more. Most new stoves are not only highly efficient but also provide a viewing glass, which has been greatly improved using a technique called an air wash, allowing a clear view of the fire even after long-term use.

WOOD PELLET STOVES AND FURNACES

When you visit your local wood stove shop, you will find pellet stoves and furnaces. A pellet stove uses wood and paper waste that would otherwise end up in the landfill. A pellet stove is an environmentally friendly replacement for your fossil fuel-fired furnace. However, a pellet stove does not qualify as a resilient heat system because it requires electricity, and the consumer has no control over the manufacturing of the pellets. If you can generate your own electricity (preferably with solar or wind energy) and store enough wood pellets, it will work; if not, you need to back up a pellet stove with a wood stove.

Fireplace Inserts

If you have an inefficient open fireplace, one that you have probably not used in quite a while, you may want to consider a fireplace insert. Most fireplace inserts, because they are recessed into a fireplace opening and chimney stack, come with an electrically operated blower to augment the radiant heat that they provide. Modern fireplace inserts have efficiencies as high as 60 percent or more, even without electricity to operate the blower. However, they are not as effective in radiating heat into a room as a free-standing wood stove simply because they are recessed. However, they fully qualify as a resilient form of backup heat. While they do not contribute a great deal of heat to the home, they can keep one or two rooms comfortably warm.

A fireplace insert with an operating electric blower will circulate heat more quickly throughout your home to compensate for heat lost when doors are opened and closed, but this is a relatively minor consideration in an emergency. One advantage an insert has over a stove is that it takes up less space. With glass doors, they can be an aesthetically pleasing addition as well as providing an effective level of resilience. However, if you open the doors to cook, you lose the airtight aspect that makes the unit efficient.

Open Fireplaces

Open fireplaces are notoriously inefficient. During the northeast ice storm of January 1998, one young couple invited their extended family (none of whom had heat) to their home, where up to twenty people gathered together in one room around a single open fireplace. As much heat was probably thrown off by twenty bodies as by the fireplace.

However, Rumford fireplaces, with a design that goes back two hundred years, are an exception. If your home happens to have a Rumford fireplace (and many do), it may be useful in a colder climate as a backup heating system, or as a primary heating system in a warmer climate. Rumfords are tall, wide, shallow, and widely angled, so that heat is radiated efficiently into the room. Such a shallow fireplace would normally tend to smoke, but Rumford rounded the breast of the chimney so that the room air coming in over the fire does not mix with the hot products of combustion, but instead goes straight up the throat of the chimney.

Because the firebox is tall, the volatile gases released by burning wood can be combusted before entering the chimney. This means less creosote buildup. It also means less pollution. With doors, some Rumford fireplaces satisfy the EPA Phase 2 criteria. Since doors reduce the amount of radiant heat, at least one company has designed a Rumford-style fireplace with a circulating heat system, where cool air is drawn from the floor, warmed by heat transfer through the firebox, and then vented back into the room. See the Web site http://www.rumford.com for more information.

A Rumford-style open fireplace with an outdoor air feed allowed a Vermont family with a young infant to continue to enjoy the comfort of their home during the ice storm. (They also had hot food and drinks courtesy of their kitchen propane range.) While the outside temperature was below freezing, the Rumford fireplace kept two core rooms at 68°F and the rest of the house at about 48°F. Although this system worked, the open fireplace consumed far more fuel than either a wood stove or an insert.

Another Vermont family with a Rumford fireplace was not as fortunate. They decided they were losing more heat up the chimney than they were gaining, so they stopped using the fireplace even though they had no other source of heat. Perhaps the difference was that their house was well insulated, and even though they had an outdoor feed to the fireplace, it was very small. Opening a window to get more air may have helped in this situation. The moral of the story: Do not simply assume your backup system will work— try it out.

If a regular fireplace is the only backup heat source you have, and you are unable to add an insert, you may be able to increase the amount of heat it generates by installing an outdoor air vent. Check with a chimney sweep to see if this would be appropriate for your fireplace. With an outdoor air vent, the fire will not rob warm air from your house in order to keep burning. If your fireplace does not have an outdoor air vent, be sure to leave a nearby window open a crack, no matter how cold it is outside. Fire needs oxygen to keep going, and so do you.

Dermot's Story

Growing up in Dublin, Ireland, I clearly recall the particular warmth of the open fireplace and range in our kitchen. We derived multiple benefits from a range fueled by an efficiently designed open coal-fired fireplace—the heat for the kitchen in which we ate our meals, the ability to cook on hot plates and bake in the oven, and a radiator at the back of the fire that brought the water in the domestic hot water tank to a boil. So, from one open fire we enjoyed cozy warmth, cooked foods, hot drinks, and hot water for bathing. Because of this wonderful fireplace, there was comfort and intimacy in that kitchen. We relaxed and were nourished in the glow of the fire's warmth. However, while the heart of the home was warm as toast, the periphery was cool to cold in winter. On many winter mornings when I was a small boy, I would wake, draw the curtains, and scrape away at the ice that had formed overnight on the inside of the window. Even though my bed was warm, my bedroom itself was cold, and getting up was something I did quickly so that I could run down to the kitchen. There the fire from the night before still glowed because we had banked it, using either coal "slack" or extra turf. Those welcome coals aglow in the grate made it easy to rekindle the fire.

Wood Furnaces

Wood furnaces, or multi-fueled furnaces that have a wood-burning capability, depend upon electricity to run the ignition system and the pump or fan required to distribute heat from the furnace. A friend and neighbor, an orchardist, heats his home entirely with a wood-fueled boiler. The boiler is located a short distance from the house next to a pile of stacked wood. The furnace is connected by an underground hot-water pipeline to the home, and thus provides heat and hot water. The system uses electric pumps to circulate the water in the heating system. When the electricity failed for six days in January, the house grew cold.

Some heating systems that use water, such as baseboard hot water, are designed so that the natural expansion of heated water circulates the water throughout the heating system on a gravity or passive distribution basis. The orchardist's system was not designed with this in mind; instead he located the furnace where it would be easy to load the wood. In this case the trade-off meant he needed an electric pump.

If you have a wood furnace that depends upon electricity, your first impulse may be to buy a backup generator. Read chapter 2 on generators first. Better yet, treat yourself to one of the electricity-free backup systems described in this chapter and the next.

Safety Precautions when Heating with Wood

We do want to stress that installing a wood-burning device must be done with the utmost attention to safety. If you already have a fireplace, stove, or insert in place, make sure they have been installed correctly. Some years ago, a neighbor asked the fire department to check out an earlier installation of a woodstove, and learned that the previous owners had used fake (flammable) brick behind the stove, and had not installed the stovepipe to the chimney correctly. Be certain that the person who installs your stove is competent and experienced. A wood stove must be placed a certain distance from walls that are flammable, and the design and installation of the chimney must be correct.

When wood is warmed, it gives off volatile gases, and it is these gases that ignite in the presence of oxygen to warm our homes. If these gases are not completely burned, they will condense on the inside of the chimney's flue, and, along with other byproducts of the fire, form a tar-like, flaky substance called creosote. A creosote buildup can block the flue and even ignite, causing fires that are extremely hot and difficult to put out.

To avoid creosote problems when using a fireplace, logs must be raised off the floor on a grate and arranged so that air can circulate under them. Otherwise the logs will just smolder without producing much heat, and the volatile gases will go up the chimney to produce creosote. For the same reason, avoid loading a stove with wood and then restricting airflow by shutting the damper. Banking a fire in this way is a common but unsafe practice. It is better to have a short, hot fire, which you then let go out. Some modern stoves or inserts are an exception: They are made to accommodate long, slow-burning fires with little creosote buildup.

Be certain to have a chimney sweep examine and clean your chimney at least once a year, preferably in the spring, or more often if you bank fires in an older stove or burn a lot of softwood. In any case, examine the chimney frequently, and have it cleaned whenever the creosote deposits are one-quarter of an inch thick.

Establish fire-drill routines, exit routes, and outdoor gathering places, and practice them with your children. Equip your home with smoke detectors, and change the batteries regularly. The fire department will be happy to give you advice on the best fire extinguisher for your needs. They will also check your fire extinguisher free of charge, and let you know when the next checkup is due. A chimney fire extinguisher is also helpful. It looks and acts like a large road flare. When struck and put into the firebox, it creates a large quantity of smoke, which smothers the fire. If you do have a chimney fire, leave the house immediately, call the fire department for help, and do not return until the firefighters say it is safe to do so.

Be sure to read the manual that comes with your wood stove, insert, or furnace, and follow its guidelines concerning the materials to use when starting a fire. Do not use the stove or insert as an incinerator, since burning treated or painted wood, magazines, and other items can release toxic chemicals into the atmosphere and your home. Certain chemicals can even damage the catalytic converter in a wood stove. The one exception is crumpled newspapers, which can be used as a base to start a fire.

Cleaning the ashes from the fireplace or stove requires some care. Be certain you have the proper tools, and follow the recommended procedures in the manual. Ashes must be carried in a metal container and stored outside in a metal can with a tight lid on a noncombustible surface such as dirt or concrete. Do not make the mistake one woman made: She threw what she thought were cold ashes on the leaf pile and found the leaves smoldering a couple of days later. Luckily, the leaves were wet.

If you have Internet access, you can find detailed information on choosing a wood-burning device, the process of starting a fire, remedies for smoking fires, safety tips, and so on, at http://www.chimney.com.

Tips for the Selection of Wood

Unless you have a chain saw, ax, and log splitter, and a private forest from which you can cut down trees, you will need to purchase wood. Here are three things to be aware of when buying wood.

The type of wood. Ask your wood supplier whether the wood is hard or soft. The denser, heavier, and harder wood is, the better it is as a source of heat. Hardwoods (from trees that lose their leaves in winter, such as maple and ash) will burn longer, leave less ash, deposit less creosote, and usually spark and smoke less than softwoods (from evergreens, such as pine and spruce). However, softwood does have its uses. It can be mixed with hardwood to make it easier to start a fire. Since wood species vary in different geographic areas, consult with a chimney sweep, wood supplier, or wood stove retailer for wood types common in your area and suitable for burning. Apple trees are typically available in most parts of the country where you might want to use wood heat, and they have a great BTU output. In addition, the wood is fragrant when burned. In an emergency, freshly cut ash will burn reasonably well. However, freshly cut elm won't burn at all, and, even when seasoned, elm is a poor source of heat.

The size of wood. Be sure the wood is sized correctly for your stove, fireplace, or furnace, as both the length and diameter influence the quality of burn and ease of use. (Ask your stove dealer for guidelines.) Do not overload the firebox. You may burn through or crack a firebox if you build a very hot fire. You will also waste fuel because there will not be enough room in the firebox for proper combustion of volatiles. Many of the heat-producing gases will simply go straight up the chimney. You can buy an inexpensive thermometer that indicates when a fire is too low, moderate, or too hot, above 500°F. These thermometers have magnets on the back so that they attach easily to your stovepipe. They are an invaluable aid for keeping your wood stove fire just right.

Time needed for seasoning. Freshly cut and split (that is, "green") wood may have a moisture content between 35 and 70 percent. The ideal moisture content for firewood is anywhere from 20 to 25 percent. Green wood does not burn as well as seasoned wood, because energy is used to eliminate the moisture in the form of steam.

To reduce the moisture content of green wood, store it under cover for a period of time, four to six months as a rule of thumb. (Check with your dealer before purchasing a particular type of wood.) If you use a tarp, cover only the top of the wood pile, leaving the sides open for ventilation.

It is easy to tell the difference between green and seasoned wood. Seasoned wood is lightweight, has dark ends, is beginning to split, and the bark peels off easily. The one exception is almond, which is very dense and heavy even when completely seasoned. Green wood is heavy and, as its name implies, often has a greenish tinge.

By choosing firewood carefully, by storing it to dry properly, and by burning it in an up-to-date stove or fireplace insert, you can reduce by about half the amount of wood needed to heat your house. And you'll be doing the environment a favor at the same time.

CHAPTER 4
HEATING WITH PROPANE, NATURAL GAS, AND OIL

An oil drilling rig alone may include ten thousand separate chips.

PRESIDENT BILL CLINTON,
*speaking to the National Academy
of Sciences, July 14, 1998*

Our utilities are all deeply dependent on software and embedded processors to operate smoothly. In order for gas and electricity to be delivered to
customers, a series of integrated parts—production facilities, transportation networks, and distribution systems—all must function properly. If
one of [these] integral parts is not Year 2000-compliant, then gas and
electricity will not be delivered to such crucial entities as hospitals,
businesses, and homes.

SENATOR DANIEL PATRICK MOYNIHAN,
*U.S. Senate Special Committee on the Year 2000
Technology Problem, June 12, 1998*

 IF YOU CANNOT OBTAIN BACKUP HEAT
with locally available resources, such as wood and
coal, or choose not to, you are left with propane, natural gas, oil, and kerosene. You may consider a number
of possible heating systems, as shown in the chart on
the next page, including the type of fuel you can use
in each one. If you choose a space heater, stove, fireplace, or fireplace
insert, make certain that it does not contain parts that require electricity to operate.

FOSSIL FUEL HEATING OPTIONS				
	Central heating with backup generator/ battery/ inverter system	Space heater /stove/insert		
		Vent through chimney	Direct vent	Vent-free
Natural Gas	X	X	X	X
Liquid Propane Gas	X	X	X	X
Oil	X	X	X	
Kerosene			X	X

Space Heaters

Each type of backup space heater, and each fuel source, has advantages and disadvantages. Consider all of these issues carefully as you determine which system best suits the needs of your home.

DIRECT-VENT HEATERS, STOVES, FIREPLACES, AND INSERTS

Today the sale of direct-vent heating units fueled by natural gas or propane accounts for two-thirds of the sales at Vermont's largest retailer of wood stoves and gas-burning fireplaces and heaters. These space heaters often copy the look and feel of wood stoves, fireplaces, and fireplace inserts, using look-alike replicas of logs and real flames. Direct vents, using outdoor air for combustion instead of warm indoor air, greatly enhance a stove's efficiency, which is one reason we recommend them over vent-free heaters. A second reason is safety; they vent to the outdoors through either an existing chimney or an outside wall, carrying exhaust fumes and vapor with them. While they may lack the romance and aroma of a real wood fire, they add a decorative element to the home, and provide useful heat output with considerably greater convenience than wood stoves.

While direct-vent heaters and wood stoves have comparable price tags, direct-vent heaters are less expensive to install. A new chimney system for a wood stove can cost from $800 to $3,000, but a direct vent for a gas-burning fireplace is as low as $200. There are two reasons for this price difference. First, a flue for a wood stove is built to withstand temperatures as high as 2,100°F, the maximum heat potential in the event of a chimney fire. Second, for proper draft, a wood stove flue needs to be two feet higher than anything within ten feet of it, including the roof. In contrast, it is easy to create a direct vent.

Some gas fireplaces are intended for decorative purposes only and provide little useful heat. Be sure to discuss your intention when talking with your local retailer. You may want a decorative fireplace, but you also want to generate BTUs to keep your family warm in an emergency.

HEATING APPLIANCES THAT USE OIL

We've identified three sources, Franco Belge, Perfection Schwank, and Enterprise, that manufacture a variety of attractive and relatively efficient space heaters, free-standing stoves, and fireplace inserts that use oil for fuel. These do not require electricity and burn regular #2 home heating oil or kerosene. The manufacturers say that they produce enough heat to warm the average home. The stoves either have a fuel reserve or can be gravity-fed from a remote oil tank as long as the tank is higher than the stove. For the homeowner who depends upon oil-fired central heating, such a system could be an ideal backup, provided that there is an adequate fuel reserve in the home. Ask your oil dealer about other electricity-free oil-burning appliances available in your locality.

NATURAL-DRAFT FIREPLACE INSERTS AND STOVES

These inserts and stoves draw air from the room and vent products of combustion up a vent pipe, which may or may not be placed inside a chimney. If you already own such an insert, by all means use it as a backup. However, if you are considering the purchase of such an item, be aware that they are not as efficient as direct-vent heaters. In addition, if your home is well insulated, or has a poorly constructed chimney, you may have downdrafts and exhaust fumes entering your home.

VENT-FREE HEATERS

While we strongly recommend a direct-vent heater, it may be better in an emergency to have some heat rather than none at all. If your budget is tight, and you have no other options, consider an unvented heater—but first check with your fire department about local ordinances and safety issues. If you do choose a vent-free heater, be aware of how dangerous they can be and follow the manufacturer's safety guidelines carefully. Use a vent-free heater in a well-ventilated area and choose a model that turns itself off if it tips over. Be sure to install top-quality carbon monoxide detectors; recently the news reported that, when tested, some carbon monoxide detectors failed to work properly. A number of people die from carbon monoxide poisoning each year. In 1997, a North Dakota family of five came close to death during a power blackout that affected thousands. They borrowed a portable propane heater from their neighbors. Although they made sure their house was properly ventilated, after only three and a half hours the heater made loud noises. They turned it off and removed it from the house. Three hours later one of the teenagers awoke with a severe headache and another felt nauseous. When the father stood up, he fell down, unconscious. It was left to fourteen-year-old Jessica to get to the phone and call for help, which soon arrived. While this story ended happily, be aware that exposure to toxic fuel vapors can be fatal.

Vent-free heating units are the fastest growing segment of the market, says Roy L'Esperance, owner of the Chimney Sweep Fireplace Shop in Shelburne, Vermont. Seventy to eighty thousand units were sold in America last year, and the numbers are growing. These units burn so effectively they can be 99.9 percent efficient, leaving no potential for carbon monoxide poisoning, as long as they are working properly. However, large amounts of moisture are a byproduct of the high efficiency. Since these units are not vented, anything settling onto the "logs" when the unit is not in use, such as dust and pet hair, burn when the flame ignites, sending the combustion byproducts directly into your house. Essentially these units are an unvented open fire in your home.

Since they have no chimney or direct vent, these units do not require professional installation. The responsibility for correct setup is yours. Be especially careful to consider clearances if you choose this type of heater. Although some say, "If you can't vent it, don't use it," it is possible to install a vent-free heater safely. Make sure there is an ample supply of fresh air in your home. One vent-free unit, made by Superia, has a catalytic converter with a glass front, which channels air to an afterburner, taking care of the chemical byproducts of the fire.

Propane and Oil Fuel Storage

The downside of gas, propane, and oil-fired backup systems or room heaters is their dependency upon a steady supply of fuel. We discussed in chapter 1 the potential for disruption of fossil fuel supplies in the event of Y2K breakdowns. If you use propane or oil, you can solve this problem by making sure that you have large enough tanks to store an adequate amount of fuel.

Determine how much fuel you use and how often your tank needs filling during each heating season. If you decide to get a larger or additional storage tank, act now. With increasing awareness of Y2K problems and the possibility of a limited fuel supply in the year 2000, prices may spike. With a generous supply of stored fuel, you can adjust your usage if necessary to last throughout the heating season.

One of our neighbors who heats with a propane-fueled fireplace decided to increase her home's resilience by storing more fuel. This gas-fired fireplace, with a 40,000 BTU input that is 80 percent efficient, had kept her home comfortably warm during a four-day power outage in January 1998. She did some research and learned that her annual propane consumption was 575 gallons. Since she intends to replace her cooking range and oven with a gas model, she will need a larger fuel reserve than her current 120-gallon tank. She decided to replace it with a 1,000-gallon tank. One propane supplier she called offered her one free 500-gallon tank and a second tank of the same size for $1,200, without telling her that 1,000-gallon tanks were also available. After additional phone calls, she found two local suppliers who were willing to provide a 1,000-gallon tank free, with a contract to sell her fuel, a common practice in this industry. She had to pay for the excavation necessary to bury the tank, but the digging itself was arranged by the supplier. Since a 1,000-gallon tank will hold about 800 gallons of propane (air takes up the rest of the space), she now feels assured of a comfortable winter.

She also learned some of the additional benefits of propane. During a power outage, you can still use a propane stove, propane refrigerator, and propane lights. According to EPA IMPACTS, which details the effects of leaks, liquid propane gas poses no threat to the natural environment. However, leaks in the home are very dangerous. Propane is flammable and must be stored properly. In comparison, oil, kerosene, and gasoline are not only flammable but also have a negative impact on the environment. These fuels are very dangerous if they leak into the ground because they can kill vegetation and contaminate groundwater and wells.

We asked a local propane supplier with nine thousand customers how much "on-site" fuel reserve they had to service their customers. Specifically, we asked, "If you do not get another delivery of gas, how long would your current supply last?" The answer was six to eight days. This Vermont company relies on daily deliveries from Canada, New York, Connecticut, and Rhode Island to replenish their propane reserves. That network is definitely vulnerable to even minor Y2K disruptions.

Natural Gas

Natural gas cannot be stored in the home, but about 90 percent of it comes from North America, which is a great advantage. While underground natural gas pipelines can withstand storms, they are not insulated from potential Y2K disruptions. If the uninterrupted use and enjoyment of your home is dependent upon the supply of fuel that arrives on demand from locations that are one or two thousand miles from your home, you should seriously consider your position. Assurances by local natural gas utilities that they are Y2K-compliant are always welcome, but gas utilities in turn depend upon others with complex technologies over which they may have little control.

It is hard to conceive of natural gas utilities failing to maintain both pressure and supply in their grid, but Y2K forces us to break conceptual barriers. We checked with our own natural gas supplier to learn more about their backup system. The natural gas for our area is piped in from Canada, and Vermont Gas Systems keeps a 5,000-gallon reserve of lique- fied propane (LP) to supplement the natural gas supply if the pressure de- creases. The pressure is monitored twenty-four hours a day, seven days a week. If a decrease in pressure is detected, the LP is mixed with natural gas at the correct temperature and amount. Only once in the last five years was this backup used. As an additional precaution, Vermont Gas has nine- teen high-volume users, who are under contract with Vermont Gas as "in- terruptible users," which means that their supply will be interrupted so that the gas can go to residential users in the event of a shortage.

While Vermont Gas System's backup measures are clearly sufficient for most emergencies, the uncertainties of Y2K, and the complex tech- nology required to pipe natural gas, indicates risk to the homeowner. Check the backup plans of the gas supplier in your area, and add a backup heating system that uses stored fuel. If this is not an option for you, make certain that your heater will function without electricity, and that there is a safety switch should the pilot light ever go out.

Details of Gas Heaters

If you choose a propane- or natural gas-fired space heater, you should fa- miliarize yourself with the following details.

EFFICIENCY
Manufacturers of gas-burning stoves and inserts often list the BTU input and output and the efficiency of the device. If the efficiency of the unit is not listed on the device, check the owner's manual for this informa- tion, or call the dealer who sold it to you. Once you have the numbers, you can estimate efficiency by dividing the heater's output by its input, and multiplying by 100. Some manufacturers claim steady-state efficien- cies for gas-fired stoves and inserts in the high 80 percent range, which is more than acceptable.

The heat output measured in BTUs of gas heaters is comparable to the heat that is generated by an equivalent-size wood stove.

IGNITION SYSTEM

Gas-fueled inserts or stoves use one of two forms of ignition. The first is a push-button system that generates its own spark to ignite a pilot light, which burns continuously and is used to ignite the main burner. The push-button system operates independently of outside electricity supply and is therefore resilient. Some such heaters are also governed by a thermostat that receives its electrical voltage (millivoltage) using a thermopile device, which generates the voltage necessary for the thermostat using the energy available from the pilot light. It actually converts pilot light heat to a minute electrical current. Such thermostat systems are also resilient.

Gas appliances can also be electronically ignited. The advantage of electronic ignition is that it eliminates the need to combust gas to keep the pilot light going during protracted periods when the appliance is not in use. The considerable disadvantage of electronic ignition is that it will not operate during electrical outages. If you currently have a gas- or oil-fired insert or stove that requires electronic ignition, check with the installer or manufacturer to see if your system can be modified. If it requires electricity, you will need either a backup generator with a battery storage bank or a backup heating system.

Oil, Gas, and Propane Furnaces

Recently, a friend told us about an older, gravity-fed, gas-fired central heating system in his mother's house in upstate New York. While this setup is less efficient than newer central heating designs, it is resilient. The gravity-circulated heating system has always operated effectively, even during fairly frequent electric outages. So when all her neighbors have lost their heat, this woman continues to enjoy the warmth and comfort of her home. If you are fortunate enough to live in such a house, then by all means keep the system, and improve it if necessary, but do not discard it. However, be sure there is an adequate supply of stored fuel at all times.

Most gas and oil central heating furnaces and boilers require electricity to ignite the burner and circulate heat. Similarly, oil-fired central heating systems require electricity to power the spray pump that injects oil into the furnace or boiler. Motors for hot-air blowers start with a requirement of around ⅛ horsepower (HP) and range up to 1 HP, depending on the size of the home and the efficiency of the heating system.

One way to add resilience to an oil heating system is to install an electric-free oil space heater. Another way is to install a generator. Before you rush out to buy a generator, read chapter 2. A generator must be dependable, sized to your family's needs, and, if fossil-fueled, have an adequate reserve of fuel. A gasoline generator may not be the best choice for your family.

CHAPTER 5

COOLING

I am genuinely concerned about the prospect of power shortages as a consequence of the millenial date change . . . I think we're no longer at the point of asking whether or not there will be any power disruptions but we are now forced to ask how severe the disruptions are going to be.

SENATOR BOB BENNETT, *chairman of the U.S. Senate Special Committee on the Year 2000 Technology Problem, June 12, 1998*

DERMOT RECOUNTS the following anecdote to illustrate the importance of home cooling: In the 1980s, my wife and I spent some time in Arkansas and unfortunately picked the beginning of a thirty-day period in which the temperature did not once fall below 100° Fahrenheit day or night. To make matters worse, the air conditioner was out of order. My wife thought that we should be able to stay cool by using our bodies' natural systems. But, late one afternoon, after a couple of days of the heat, the likes of which my cold-acclimated Irish blood had never before experienced, I felt unwell and weak and went to bed. I soon lost consciousness and could not be roused by my wife.

That evening and night the temperature in the house dropped from the daytime high of 114°F to about 100°F. Realizing that she needed to cool my body, my wife applied cold compresses to my unconscious frame. She also had the air conditioner fixed. It was good that she acted, because I had heatstroke, from which I could have died.

People routinely do die during heat waves. In a normal year, 175

heat-related deaths occur in the United States. Statistics from the National Weather Service show that 1,021 heat-related fatalities and 1,549 heat-related injuries occured in 1995, the largest death toll of any natural disaster. Damage from the heat wave that year totaled about $500 million. During the summer of 1998, the mercury stayed above 100°F for weeks in the south-central portion of the country, causing, as of mid-summer, 146 deaths, with 99 in Texas alone. Most of the victims were elderly women and men who, determined to get by without air conditioning, mistakenly believed that this summer was just like any other. In fact, Texas experienced fifty-eight straight days of 100°F-plus readings, making the summer of 1998 even hotter than 1980, which had forty-two consecutive days when the mercury rose above 100°F. Dallas County health officials declared a state of emergency and other counties across the state sought federal disaster assistance to compensate for losses of more than $1.5 billion in farming and ranching. Florida suffered from an unusually severe drought and resulting forest fires that caused hundreds of millions of dollars in damage to over 700 square miles of land in residential and rural areas. Coupled with heavy rains in California, Arizona, and Iowa, and way above-average temperatures in North Dakota, Arkansas, and Oregon, 1998 may go down as the year with the weirdest weather in a decade.

All this appears to be a warning that global warming is here to stay, according to scientists on the Intergovernmental Panel on Climate Change at the United Nations, who expect global temperatures to rise between two and six degrees in the next century. And, because excessive heat is no joke, it has become imperative for all of us to find ways to protect ourselves from hot weather.

If you live in a hot and humid climate, or have a low tolerance for heat, your ability to stay in your home without becoming ill during a power failure may be limited, if you cool your house with air conditioners run by electricity from the power grid. Whether the problem is caused by an earthquake, tornado, hurricane, flood, or Y2K power interruptions, if you are without electricity for days or weeks, your home will quickly become unlivable during the summer.

The core vulnerability for hot climates is the fact that virtually all cooling devices require electricity. Even natural gas-fired heat pumps or air conditioners require electricity for fans and ignition. Over the years, our electrical infrastructure has been so reliable that any temporary inconvenience from a power outage has not been an undue burden.

Cooling Is More than a Luxury

Artificial cooling is a relatively recent phenomenon, and was probably driven initially by comfort considerations rather than absolute need. In the deep South, for example, plantation homes remained relatively cool because they were shaded by large trees, had high ceilings and covered verandahs, and were surrounded by vegetation and open space, which permitted the free passage of air around and into the house.

But today many of us live in small homes placed close together, so that natural breezes cannot flow freely. Many lots, particularly in tract developments, have been stripped of all their shade trees. What's more, we work in modern office buildings totally dependent on electric power for heating and cooling. Acres of tar-and-concrete-covered land in our suburbs and cities attract and hold heat. Because of these factors, our cooling needs have increased.

On the plus side, brick or masonry have a greater thermal mass than other construction materials. In warmer climates, if the ventilation is good, a house constructed of brick or masonry will remain as cool as the proverbial cucumber and thus more comfortable than conventionally built wood-frame structures, because the transfer of solar heat to the interior is slower, resulting in less heat buildup and lower temperatures.

To prepare for possible interruptions in power, and to lower your cooling costs during normal operations as well, you can take a number of steps to take advantage of natural cooling. These techniques come under the general category of "passive cooling."

Passive Cooling

Passive cooling has been used by humans—and animals—for centuries. In addition to the plantation houses in the southeast, indigenous tribes in the southwest lived in caves that were functional, cool, comfortable, hospitable, and sometimes quite elaborate.

In all passive cooling, the most important thing you can do is keep the heat out in the first place. Adequate insulation is essential; other passive cooling techniques involve landscaping, shading, and ventilation.

INSULATION

Insulating your home is a must because it keeps you comfortable and saves money by decreasing the need for cooling in summer and heating in winter. If you haven't checked the insulation level recently, now would be an excellent time to decide whether you need to add some. A qualified home energy auditor will include an insulation check as a routine part of an energy audit. The areas to check are the attic, ceilings, exterior and interior basement walls, and crawl spaces. If you want to perform an energy audit yourself, send for the Department of Energy booklet DOE/CE-0180 (dated August 1997), and/or booklet DOE/GO-10097-431 (dated September 1997), by writing to the U.S. Department of Energy, Office of Technical Information, PO Box 62, Oak Ridge, TN 37831; by calling them at 423-576-2286 or 576-8401; or by visiting their Web site at http://www.ornl.gov/roofs+walls or http://www.eren.doe.gov. (See chapter 3 for more information on insulation.)

LANDSCAPING

Planting trees is not practical between now and the year 2000 because it takes too long for a new tree to grow tall enough to shade your house. But shrubbery located a few feet away from the house, if placed to take advantage of prevailing winds, will funnel cooling air currents into your house. In fact, the book *Energy-Efficient and Environmental Landscaping* by Anne Simon Moffat, Marc Schiler, and the staff of Green Living (Appropriate Solutions, 1994; distributed by Chelsea Green) states, "on the same day, at the same time, at only slightly different locations, landscaping can change the temperature by 20° to 25°F." You can also shade the most vulnerable rooms, those facing south and west, by installing trellises and covering them with fast-growing vines. Check with a local nursery for the appropriate plants for your area and let nature help cool your house. To avoid losing heat from the Sun in winter, it might be a good idea to choose vines that lose their leaves during the coolest months.

Trees and vines have the additional advantage of creating a cool microclimate that can dramatically reduce temperature by as much as 9°F.

This is because large quantities of water vapor escape through the leaves during photosynthesis, cooling the passing air, and because dark, coarse leaves absorb solar radiation, protecting your house. And there is finally some good news for the American lawn much beleaguered by critics who claim they're ecologically dubious. A grass-covered lawn is 10°F cooler than bare ground in summer. A wildflower meadow may be even cooler.

SHADING

If a trellis does not appeal to you or will not work for your home, you can install awnings, louvers, shutters, or shades outside, or use solar screens or specially designed interior shades with backings that absorb heat. Exterior shading is the most beneficial because it stops the heat before it gets to the windows. Of the various shading options, awnings are the most effective heat barriers, particularly light-colored ones that reflect sunlight, because they can reduce heat build-up by 65 percent on southern windows and 77 percent on eastern ones. Louvered awnings have adjustable slats that can control the amount of sun in the home, while shutters can be slatted or solid. Anyone who has ever visited Italy or Spain during the summer can testify to the effectiveness of those heavy shutters that, when closed, keep interior rooms cool even while the Sun is blazing. All these options, however, do block the view and solid shutters can stop airflow, so be sure to buy the slatted variety if airflow is important to you. Solar screens are interior shades that do not block the view. They look like regular screens but prevent direct sunlight from entering the room, cut glare, and preserve airflow. Other methods of interior shading include draperies and curtains, Venetian blinds, honeycombed shades with mylar coating (which have the added benefit of an R-value), and opaque roller shades.

Although it doesn't exactly qualify as shading, another important consideration in keeping your house cool is paint. If your house needs painting, make sure you use a light color on the exterior, which absorbs less heat than dark colors.

VENTILATION

Proper ventilation is one of the most important aspects of passive cooling because the movement of air evaporates perspiration and cools the body. If you compare a room at 85°F with no air movement to one at the same temperature but with plenty of ventilation, the effective temperature your body feels will be 5° lower in the ventilated room. Ideal rooms have windows on opposite walls, which permit cross-ventilation as breezes enter and leave freely. Attic vents should be installed to provide one inch of ventilation space between the insulation and the roofing material. They can be placed along the entire ceiling cavity to provide proper airflow. Make sure your contractor does not block these vents with insulation.

Roofs are a major problem, as about one-third of the unwanted heat in your house comes through the roof and is stored in the attic. Reflective roof-coating materials are available at your local hardware store, which you can apply yourself or hire a professional to install. One is white latex, which is suitable for many roofing materials, including asphalt and fiberglass shingles, tar paper, and metal. A second is asphalt-based with glass fibers and aluminum particles and works with most metal and asphalt roofs. It is sticky, however, which attracts dust and reduces its reflectivity slightly. Another less expensive technique is to install a radiant barrier, which is really a sheet of aluminum foil with paper backing, under the insulation of your roof. If installed correctly, this will cut heat accumulation by 25 percent. Installing vents in a roof that does not already have them, or does not have enough of them, helps move the hot attic air out. A good rule of thumb in determining how much roof venting you need is to allow one square foot of unobstructed opening for every 300 square feet of roof area. If you happen to be building a new house, look into a double-skinned (or ventilated-skin) roof. The vented area allows heated air to rise and exit at the peak in the roof, while cooler outside air enters through vents at the bottom of the roof. Insulation is placed under the second skin. This type of construction can be used in walls as well.

Other Things to Keep Cool

In extreme heat before the era of air conditioning, one effective way to cool off was to get into a cold bath. Bev remembers one heat wave in the

1940s, when the mercury climbed to 106°F in the city, when cold baths were a major survival technique.

Another approach is to reduce the sources that generate heat within your house, such as lights, stove and oven, dishwasher, washer, dryer, and refrigerator. You can lessen the heat of incandescent bulbs by switching to compact fluorescent bulbs, which use 75 percent less energy and emit 90 percent less heat. They may seem incredibly expensive, but because they last so much longer than incandescent bulbs and use so much less electricity, they are not; in fact, they save money over the life of the bulb. Use appliances such as the washer and dryer early in the morning or late at night when it is coolest and when electric rates tend to be lowest. Put up a clothesline and dry your clothes outside, a simple use of solar energy and one that makes your wash smell better than any detergent fragrance. Use your outdoor barbecue instead of the stove to cook on hot days. And consider replacing old, energy-expensive appliances with new energy-efficient ones. This is particularly true for refrigerators, as the older models give off a great deal of heat.

As far as your air conditioning system goes, there is not too much you can do if the electricity is out. One idea is to use a backup generator to operate just the air conditioner. In an emergency, you can restrict your living quarters and therefore reduce the number of hours the air conditioner operates, and you will have a comfortable envelope in an otherwise overheated house; this will also allow you to stretch out your store of fuel for the generator.

Another idea is to have a modest battery backup system with an inverter and use the battery power to operate electric fans, which consume much less electricity than air conditioners. Recharge the battery when the power is on. This method is useful in rolling blackouts, which occur when the electric capacity is strained and there is not enough power to service all areas all the time (see chapter 1). The battery system can be used with or without a generator, and can be as large or small as you choose. Be sure to work with an electrician for the safe installation of any reserve system that interfaces with the electrical panels in your house.

CHAPTER 6
FOOD

It might not be a bad idea to have a little extra food and water around in case the supermarket can't get its stocks for 72 hours or a week or two because of breakdowns in the transportation system.

SENATOR BOB BENNETT,
*chairman of the U.S. Senate Special Committee
on the Year 2000 Technology Problem,
speaking to the National Press Club, July 15, 1998*

 FOR MANY YEARS, we have enjoyed a splendid abundance of food in the U.S. Without discounting the reality of poverty, for the most part we have come to expect that we will always have food, no matter how far it has to travel to get to us, or how complex and computer-dependent the processing and distribution paths may be. Y2K is our wakeup call. In truth, our food supply depends upon a massive and complex system, not unlike the infrastructure of the electric utility industry, and is as vulnerable to Y2K, and to other mishaps as well.

For example, food in the U.S. travels an average of 1,300 miles from farm to store shelf. Almost every state buys 85 to 90 percent of its food from someplace else. The average U.S. city has only a three-day supply of food in supermarkets and grocery stores, and that supply depends upon an elaborate network of growing, processing, packing, refrigerating, transporting, and selling, all of which is orchestrated and controlled by computer programs and machines salted with date-sensitive embedded chips. If the Y2K bug were to damage the network in one place, it is unlikely the whole system would collapse, but regional failures affecting your local supermarket could occur. On the plus side, teams of experts

are working to resolve the issue, and the U.S. Department of Transportation has contacted companies worldwide, informing them of the risks to ports and ships, and to road and rail transportation.

Y2K as Opportunity

Imagine how different things would be if most foods were produced and consumed within the same locale. For example, juice from apples grown and processed in California would not be sent to the East Coast but would be consumed locally, while people in the east would drink juice from apples grown in their area. This would avoid the cost of transporting food over great distances, including the hidden costs to our environment and health.

In this ideal scenario, a federal carbon tax could be imposed on fossil fuel, resulting in an increase in fuel prices. This would discourage long-distance food transport and stimulate local agriculture and local consumption. Due to climate, it might take time to develop a local food supply, perhaps using greenhouses. Arrangements would have to be made to alleviate the impact of the fossil fuel tax on low-income families.

Community Supported Agriculture

Even before Y2K became a national issue, many far-sighted communities have taken an interest in promoting home gardening and other forms of local food production, such as community supported agriculture (CSA). CSA is an increasingly popular method that allows consumers to develop a relationship with local producers. The consumer works with a farmer and provides capital by buying shares, essentially a method of pre-payment or partial pre-payment, in exchange for a portion of the farmer's crop. There are variations on this basic theme.

The beauties of CSA are many: It helps bring our eating patterns back into alignment with locally available, seasonal food that is fresh and nutritious; it reduces the energy resources consumed in the food system;

it creates a sense of community; and it helps local farmers. When you, the consumer, come into closer contact with the producer, you have a greater say in how your food is grown. For example, you can choose to finance the work of an organic farmer, thus avoiding pesticides, chemical fertilizers, and genetically engineered food. In this connection, it is important to note that 60 percent of all soy bean plants grown in the U.S. now have built-in pesticides.

More than 600 CSAs already operate in the U.S. and Canada and the number is growing rapidly. If one does not exist in your area, consider helping to start one. In addition to CSA farms, you can hook up with other local networks of food production and distribution, such as food cooperatives. Participants often work in the retail store and have a say about how their food is grown and distributed. In the short-term, participating in these local food networks can improve your ability to manage during Y2K disruptions or other emergencies. In the long-term, strengthening these networks is good for communities and the planet.

Home Gardening

Sixty million Americans can't be wrong. That is the number of people gardening in the United States today. If you are not one of them, now is a good time to sharpen your growing skills, and not only because of Y2K. Growing your own food is cheaper than buying it; gives you control over its quality because you can avoid pesticides and herbicides, thereby producing healthier food; brings you closer to nature; gives you fresh air, exercise, and vitamin D when the Sun is out, which you need to absorb calcium; is Earth-friendly because it consumes far less energy than the tractors and combines employed by agribusiness; and reduces the influence of the far-flung, tenuous, and computer-controlled corporate food system.

Anyone can grow vegetables because it is easy. It is also very satisfying. If you have never put a seed into the ground and flushed with joy when it actually came up, new pleasures are in store for you. A number of vegetables are particularly easy to grow—lettuce, spinach, broccoli, tomatoes, carrots, green beans, and peppers. Also trouble-free are several herbs: Thyme, tarragon, and oregano are perennials in many climates, and parsley and basil are annuals that love sun. Gardening is a good family activity as children can help once they are old enough to learn the difference between a plant and a weed. Even city apartment dwellers can grow vegetables in window boxes and pots on their terraces or roofs. Suburbanites can set aside a portion of the yard for a vegetable garden, at the same time reducing the need to mow the grass. If you have the space, you can create a composting bin for leaves, grass cuttings, weeds, and kitchen waste (exclusive of meat and fish scraps because they attract animals), reducing the wear and tear on your garbage disposal and the amount of waste going to the landfill. Composting is as easy as growing plants. Best of all, when you add compost to your vegetable garden, you automatically enrich the soil.

An excellent guide to home gardening is *Passport to Gardening* by Katherine LaLiberté and Ben Watson, which helps you find the resources to build healthy soil, start composting, use water efficiently, save seeds, control pests and plant diseases, and grow all manner of vegetables, herbs, and fruits (as well as flowers).

Ah-ha, you say, that is all very well and good for spring and summer, and for folks who live in the South, but what about people in the northern tier of our country? The good news is that you can harvest foods throughout the year in the north using all manner of covered gardens—cold frames, tunnels, and root cellars. You can grow root crops for storage in winter—carrots, potatoes, cabbage, beets, onions, and garlic. These vegetables store reasonably well in any cool, dark place; you do not need to create an elaborate root cellar. An excellent book to guide you through year-round gardening is *Four-Season Harvest* by Elliot Coleman. Yet another resource is *Keeping Food Fresh*, from the organic gardeners of Terre Vivante, an ecological center south of Grenoble, France, which describes old-world techniques for preserving food that were familiar to our forebears but have been forgotten by our modern society enraptured with energy-intensive canning and freezing.

Local production of food has been a theme of leaders and luminaries who have expounded the concept and principles of sustainability, such as E. F. Shumacher, Amory Lovins, and Lyman Wood. Shumacher wrote of the folly of transporting biscuits (cookies, to us) manufactured in Southern England to Northern England, while at the same time transporting biscuits manufactured in Northern England to Southern England. Amory Lovins grows bananas at 8,000 feet in the Rocky Mountains, and all the energy that his home and office require comes from solar and other renewable energy sources. Lyman Wood, founder of Garden Way Associates, located a multi-million-dollar international company headquarters in a log cabin next to his rural home, leaving room for his garden, which produced an abundance of fresh vegetables. Promoting gardening was a theme that ran like a thread through all of his activities, and he stressed the recreational and health benefits of growing at least some of your own food. A second theme in Lyman's life was business "not-for-profit" only, and his generosity of spirit and financial contribution fueled the growth of the National Gardening Association, which promotes gardening in the homes, inner cities, jails, and schools of America.

Be Pro-active

There are two fundamental ways to respond to Y2K in terms of storing food. The first is fear-based, with a view to "surviving" until things are back to normal, or the world as we know it has ended, whichever comes first. The second is a reasoned response, with a view to creating a long-term pantry (or root cellar) that will serve you well not only during any disruptions caused by Y2K, but also when bad weather makes it hard to get to the store. Not so long ago, it was the norm for people to have a pantry, or reasonable store of food, as they headed into the winter.

The idea that the United States of America might lack food in any way is almost unimaginable. Ironically, fear could result in hoarding and could lead to shortages, especially of certain items, such as coffee. The wonderful economist Amartya Sen, who received the Nobel Prize in economics in 1998, has spent much of his career studying food shortages and famines. He experienced famine firsthand as a child in Bangladesh. He has shown in his work that famines often have as much to do with panic as with weather and the harvest.

Y2K and the Food Supply

How serious is the problem? U.S. Secretary of Agriculture Dan Glickman says that the Food Supply Working Group "is committed to assuring that everyone involved in food supply production and distribution is aware of potential Y2K problems, understands the importance of acting now to check their systems, and knows where they can go for help. Our goal: to do whatever we can to prevent any disruption in the food supply chain come January 1, 2000."

That's the good news. But it is important to understand that food suppliers, like so many businesses, are heavily dependent on computerized processing and information exchange and date-sensitive embedded chips. For example, farmers and ranchers who use automated harvesting, feeding, watering, and milking equipment; food processors whose production and packaging assembly lines, billing systems, and truck refrigeration systems are computer-dependent; and food retailers who rely on computers for ordering, inventory control, refrigerating, and registering sales; all are vulnerable to Y2K failures. Other problems could arise among those who supply needed goods and services to the agricultural industry: fertilizer and pesticide manufacturers; gasoline producers, refiners, and distributors; and electricity generators, suppliers, and distributors.

Extended power failures can cause major food spoilage resulting from failure of computer-operated food storage refrigeration or delivery systems. Since we now import more than 50 percent of our oil from countries that are unlikely to be Y2K-compliant by the year 2000, this adds another level of vulnerability.

In addition, all sectors of the food production and distribution system are vulnerable to power outages caused by Y2K failures, especially outages lasting more than a few days, which would exhaust backup systems and cause foods needing refrigeration to spoil.

What is more, the problem goes beyond computers. Equipment containing time-dependent embedded computer chips is at risk: harvesting equipment, milking machinery, grain elevators, plant and truck refrigeration systems, store and plant security systems, grocery and restaurant cash registers, telephones, gas and water facilities, and plant assembly lines.

What is the federal government doing about food-related Y2K problems? Most recently, through the President's Council on Year 2000 Conversion, federal agencies are reaching out to domestic and international organizations to increase awareness of the situation and to offer support. For example, the Departments of Agriculture, Defense, Health and Human Services, State, and the Commodity Futures Trading Commission have been asked by the council to coordinate an outreach campaign in the food sector because all have food-sector constituencies.

All this should convince you that growing your own food and preserving the excess produce for later use, as well as storing basic staples and water, are excellent ideas. Another factor to consider in this complex mix is California, the nation's salad bowl, which supplies 50 percent of all our fruits and vegetables. The state is prone to earthquakes, mud slides, flood, and drought; any of these natural disasters could impact the supply of food.

In the last one hundred years, food production in the United States has undergone an enormous change. According to the U.S. Census Bureau, it took 42 percent of the population to produce enough food to feed the nation in 1900, while today approximately 2 percent of us produce enough to feed everyone. This miracle never could have happened without the industrialization of agriculture and the use of computers.

As a result of this consolidation of food production, 90 percent of the food most Americans eat travels a considerable distance from the growing fields of California, the Midwest, Southwest, and Southeast to the rest of the country. We enjoy eating three times a day, and we need at least one or two solid meals per day to survive over the long haul. Because the system that supplies food to grocery stores around the nation is highly efficient, we tend to take well-stocked supermarkets for granted. But this may be false confidence.

It may seem unlikely that the food supply might be disrupted—but it has happened before. Bev remembers the time she walked into an American supermarket and found—to her great shock—no meat for sale. This was in Maine during the summer of 1973 or 1974 and she had five children to feed, four of them teenagers, in addition to assorted adult houseguests. Turkeys were available, and for one solid month that summer they ate turkey, along with beans and vegetables.

The supermarket manager thought it had something to do with the sharp rise in the price of oil due to the Arab oil boycott, which had disrupted transportation. Bev and her family could not believe this was happening in the United States, the land of such plentiful food that visitors from other parts of the world were amazed at the quantity and variety of the meals she served them. In those days, the American public was not aware that avoiding red meat provided cholesterol-lowering health benefits, and so everyone groused a lot. For the boys in particular, the absence of hamburgers signaled the end of the world.

What is true for supermarkets also applies to restaurants, particularly fast-food franchises. According to the information service of the National Restaurant Association, 44 percent of the total amount spent on food in this country goes to restaurants. What is more, on any given day, according to Catherine E. Woteki, Acting Undersecretary for Research, Education and Economics at the United States Department of Agriculture (USDA), 57 percent of Americans consumed meals and snacks away from home in 1994–1995. "Seventeen years ago, by comparison," she pointed out, "43 percent of Americans ate away from home. Given the prevalence of two-career families, the lack of time available for home cooking, and the wide variety of choices available for meals away from home, the increase is not surprising." It probably explains one joke making the rounds among baby-boomer families that goes something like this: Ask an eight year old what she wants for her birthday and she'll say "a home-cooked meal."

Thus, potential supply problems may fall across the entire groaning board if Y2K computer malfunctions interrupt our food supply.

An Imaginary Walk

Imagine you are in the north in the depths of winter, and the Y2K bug or some other disaster disrupts the supply of food. Checking your cupboards, you find approximately a week's worth of groceries. Unable to predict the length of the disruption, you and everyone else in town descends upon the local grocery stores to ensure that you have the necessary items to feed your family. As a result, the stores are cleared out in a matter of days, or even hours.

Let's say that you succeed in purchasing an additional week's worth of food. This is highly unlikely because of the limited food supply in your neighborhood stores. But for argument's sake, let's assume you now have a two-week supply of food. Then let's imagine the worst—that the emergency lasts longer than that. What do you do to acquire food in the middle of winter, surrounded by snow, ice, and freezing conditions, where nothing grows? It is obvious that the four-season approach to gardening noted above would be a life saver if you found yourself in this position. Even if you live in the Deep South, if water and electricity supplies are disrupted, there will be no irrigation to keep your garden, or the farmers' fields, alive.

We hope that no disruptions in the food supply will occur, but instead of taking chances, make your home resilient. Consider growing some vegetables for immediate consumption and for storage. Plan to store one month's supply (or more) of food. And add extra for your neighbor.

Food Storage

There are two strategies for food storage. The first is to purchase an amount of food and put it entirely aside as a reserve. A drawback to this method is that all foods have a limited shelf life: after a certain period of time they must be discarded for safety's sake. The second strategy is to rotate stored food, so that as food is used from the stored supply you replace it. With either strategy, be sure to choose foods your family likes to eat, and include some snacks. Remember to store enough food for a baby's special needs and also for others with special dietary requirements. In the event of a water shortage that makes dishwashing impossible, it is important to have on hand paper cups, plates, napkins, and towels; and plastic eating utensils, moistened towelettes, and trash bags.

Since an electrical shutdown will put refrigerators and freezers out of commission, fresh and frozen foods are not suitable for storage during an emergency. Choose food to store from the following categories:

- *Canned goods* are readily available—soup, meat, rice, pasta, vegetables, and fruit. Make a point to buy extra cans of whatever you normally purchase to dedicate to your emergency supply. Date the top of anything stored with a black permanent marker. Plan for a minimum of three cans per person per day, and multiply that by the number of days you want your storage cache to cover. Remember that canned goods with moisture content, like ready-to-eat soup, will help meet your need for liquids, but may not be as filling as solid foods. Be sure there is a manual can opener in the house; if there is no power, your electric can opener will be useless.

Pay close attention to how the packaging holds up in damp environments. Cans will rust unless protected. A good way to prevent rusted cans is to put them in a zipper bag, and then pack them inside a food-grade plastic bucket with a lid.

- If you can cook over a wood stove or other resilient appliance, consider adding *staples* to your canned goods supply. Rice, beans, grains, cereals, noodles, and flour are good to have on hand. Sugar, salt, pepper, herbs, spices, coffee, and tea add variety to your diet. Also include jars of peanut butter, honey, jam and jelly, crackers, vacuum-packed nuts, and dried fruits.
- *Freeze-dried and air-dried (dehydrated) foods* can also become part of your food storage plan. Dried fruits are an excellent source of calories. You can readily obtain powdered milk, soups, potatoes, and other items from your local grocery store. Or you can buy a variety of dehydrated foods in one-gallon (#10) cans. Properly stored, dehydrated food has one splendid advantage: a ten- to fifteen-year shelf life.

Don't forget your pets. If you store canned food for your pet, review the precautions under canned goods above. Or store, use, and replace as you would your own food.

FOODS PREPARED FOR STORAGE

A number of companies sell various kinds of packaged foods for storage, which we describe below. Before Y2K, the market for these foods was relatively small. Since their production capacity is limited, some of these products are already on back order. If you favor this type of food storage, it would be wise to order whatever you need as soon as possible.

MREs (meals ready to eat) require no cooking—just open the package and eat. They are ideal for outside storage as they survive unspoiled in the worst conditions. They also have a long shelf life so that you don't have to rotate your supply. Consider, though, that MREs contain highly processed food of dubious nutritional value. Most of these meals include a meat entree, pound cake, and usually an additional item, such as applesauce or potatoes au gratin, plus the famous accessory pack of salt, pepper, a beverage, toilet paper, matches, sauce, and spoons. Each meal contains 1,300 to 1,500 calories. There are six varieties; some come with more, others with less meat. Each case contains twelve meal packs. You can order them by calling 1-800-321-2900; their average cost is about $69 a case plus shipping and handling, though you can get a discount by ordering two or more cases and an even bigger break for large orders.

Emergency food bars are good storage items because each pre-packaged meal provides a nutritional balance of vitamins and minerals and has a shelf life of five years. Each packet weighs 1½ pounds and contains nine 400-calorie bars, or 3,600 calories in all. Currently, "Mainstay" is the only emergency food developed specifically for both land-based and marine use. These food bars do not provoke thirst, nor do they contain cholesterol or tropical oils. The bars meet strict Jewish and Islamic dietary requirements, and are protected in durable, waterproof, vacuum-sealed packaging to withstand temperatures ranging from -40°F to 300°F. What's more, these bars are approved by the U.S. Defense Personnel Support Center, UN agencies, and the Food Engineering Directorate of the U.S. Army and U.S. Coast Guard. A case contains ten packets and costs $69.95. They are available from Aquacheck, whose toll-free number in the continental U.S. is 1-800-504-5580. Outside of the continental U.S. the number is 714-739-7755.

A book containing comprehensive information about food storage is *Making the Best of Basics* by James Talmage Stevens. It covers what you may need in the way of food and water, where to get it, how to store it, and how to cook using wheat, bulgur wheat, sourdough, and white flour, dairy products, and honey. There are sections on kitchen gardening, sprouting, and drying foods, and a section devoted to companies that sell foods suitable for storage (organized by state). It also has easy-to-use charts to guide your efforts.

Cooking

Electric stoves obviously will not be useful during a power failure. Gas stoves may or may not work, depending on your reserve supply and whether or not the gas company is functioning. You can cook on top of a wood stove very effectively, as Bev discovered during the ice storm, when she made spaghetti sauce and turkey soup, among other foods. But she also discovered why someone invented kitchens. Her most efficient wood stove happens to be in her bedroom, so she went to sleep feeling she was inside her oven while dinner was being prepared.

If you have an open fireplace, you can cook in it the way our ancestors did. Remember all the eighteenth-century villages you have visited with the cast-iron pots hanging on hooks above the fireplace and try to rig up something similar.

If you can venture outside, that is, if it is not –20°F, you can cook on your charcoal or gas barbecue or camp stove. But be sure not to bring them inside, because they emit carbon monoxide, which can be deadly. If you own or have access to a recreational vehicle or a boat, you can use the RV or marine stove.

Having considered and planned for your family's emergency food needs, you can enjoy the peace of mind that comes with being ready. There is no better stress-reduction formula than knowing your family will not go hungry even if the power companies are not functioning and the supermarkets are empty. The old Boy Scout motto—Be Prepared— certainly applies to food with Y2K just around the corner.

CHAPTER 7

WATER AND SANITATION

> I think water will be available in most municipalities, but I am convinced there are some where the water system will break down. And there could be serious, serious difficulty in those communities.
>
> SENATOR BOB BENNETT,
> *chairman of the U.S. Senate Special Committee*
> *on the Year 2000 Technology Problem,*
> *speaking to the National Press Club, July 15, 1998*

 WHILE CHANGING WEATHER PATTERNS can create floods and droughts that affect our local water supply, Y2K will not at all influence the quantity of available water. But it may alter the capacity of municipal systems to deliver water and ensure its quality. Sanitation services may also be at risk. Even if you have a well, if there is a power failure in your community, the electric pump that brings water from the well to the household pipes will not work.

Water

According to the American Waterworks Association, the average American consumes 86.2 gallons of water per day: drinking, showering, washing clothes and dishes, cooking, flushing the toilet, and watering the lawn. We are a water-consuming society and water use has been growing exponentially. Total water withdrawals in the United States have jumped from 140 billion gallons in 1940 to 408 billion gallons today. All this is occurring while our supply of fresh water is diminishing, as we empty the underground aquifers that supply our water faster than nature can restore them.

Thus, while you prepare for a possible water shortage in your home, you may want to consider a permanent reduction in your water consumption as well. Some older toilets use between five and seven gallons of water every time you flush. This would be a good time to install a more efficient toilet that only uses one and one-half gallons of water per flush. Inexpensive, low-flow valves for shower heads and aerators for kitchen and bathroom faucets break the water into a fine, effective spray. Front-load washing machines that tumble the clothes, instead of agitating them, require much less water to clean clothes effectively, and are gentler as well. If you are planning to buy a washing machine anytime soon, be certain to check out these models.

During an emergency, of course, you may need to limit your use of water even further. Next to oxygen, water for drinking is our most essential need. You can live for weeks without food but only a few days without drinking water. Your body needs water to keep its organs, joints, and muscles well lubricated, as well as to digest food. What's more, without water, the electrical balance in your body's cells loses its equilibrium, causing serious disruptions in many bodily systems.

If You Have a Well

If you have your own well, the pump will not work if the electricity goes out. One solution is to buy a backup generator to provide the electricity you need, and to store an adequate amount of fuel. Another solution is to use a solar cell to supply power to either an AC or DC submersible pump. Real Goods (1-800-919-2400) offers a solar submersible pump kit for just under $1,600 (see chapter 2). Alternatively, you can install a hand pump, which requires human energy to operate.

It is a common belief that hand pumps only work for shallow wells; one pump supplier said that we would need the power of three horses to pump domestic water from a depth of more than 20 feet. However, at least one company manufactures hand pumps for domestic wells that are effective down to depths of 200 feet. These pumps have a stroke length

that can be adjusted from 5 inches to 7.5 inches to 10 inches by sliding a pin into different holes. With a two-inch cylinder, water can be reached at the following depths with different length pump strokes: at 200 feet deep with a 5-inch pump stroke; at 140 feet with a 7.5-inch pump stroke; and at 108 feet deep with a 10-inch pump stroke. With a larger diameter, say four inches, the pump cannot draw water from as great a depth. For example, a 5-inch pump stroke draws water from only 62 feet, the 7.5 inch from 43 feet, and the 10 inch from 33 feet. The company that manufactures these pumps is called Monitor (a division of Baker Manufacturing Co., Evansville, WI 53536; 608-882-2730). Monitor celebrated its 125th anniversary as a manual pump manufacturer in 1998; to say that its pumps are tried and true is perhaps an understatement.

These manual pumps will fit into many existing wells if the well access is six inches or more in diameter. If it is, the cylinder can be inserted without getting in the way of the existing submersible electric pump and associated lines. If suitable for your well, a backup hand pump will provide a reasonable amount of water for drinking and some other purposes, sufficient to allow you to continue living in your home and enjoying some of its comforts. You can call Baker's technical support number (800-356-5130) to discuss your needs and decide if you can install the pump yourself, or if you need to hire a plumber.

To determine what capacity pump you need, measure the distance from the ground down to the level that water rises to in the well, which is called the static level. According to Monitor's catalog, a hand pump and fittings for a deep well would cost $500 to $800 depending on the static level of the well.

One caution: Manual pumps can freeze in colder climates. To avoid this, a draining "weep" hole is drilled at the frost line, but pumps can and do freeze in some circumstances. Pouring warm water over the pump thaws any frozen water at the level of the pump; however, the freeze could be deeper. Monitor also makes a less expensive hand pump ($288.50) suitable for a shallow well with a static level of up to 25 feet. Rintoul's Hand Pumps (519-596-2612; www.handpumps.com) distributes the Sigma, a hand pump for a well with a static head of 22 feet, for $120. Another supplier of hand pumps is The Bosworth Company (888-438-1110).

Kitchen or "pitcher" pumps can retrieve water from shallow wells or cisterns with a static level of up to 20 feet. They are small, simple to use, and inexpensive, costing about $60, excluding whatever piping is needed. They work by creating a vacuum. When you put an intake pipe into the water supply and drive a handle up and down, the vacuum created sucks the water into the pipe and the pump sends it to a bucket or sink. These small pumps require little maintenance and last for years.

Sump Pumps

The Monitor pump for shallow wells can be used as a backup system for a sump pump, if you are concerned about the possibility of a flooded basement. To determine the capacity of the pump you need, consider how quickly water collects in the basement, the amount of water that must be pumped, and the lift or head (vertical distance) that the water must travel to the outside. With this information in hand, you can choose a pump suitable to your needs.

The Bosworth Company makes a pump called the Guzzler, which sells for $48 to $60 (not including accessories) that can be used to eliminate basement water. The Guzzler comes in two series; choose one depending on the amount of water to be moved. For example, the 400 series, with a hose diameter of 1 inch, will move 10 gallons of water a minute, while the 500 series uses a hose that measures 1.5 inches and moves 15 gallons a minute. (Garden hoses are not suitable because they are too narrow.) If you are pumping from the basement, run the hose out a window onto the lawn where the grade slopes away from the house. The average person will have no problem operating the hand pump. The Guzzler can also be used for wells with a static level of 12 feet or less.

Municipal Water Supply

Have you ever wondered exactly how the water you take for granted gets to your house, your business, the local health club, all the restaurants in town, and the schools? We decided to investigate the source of water in our area, which is probably typical for many towns in the United States.

Our water comes from Lake Champlain and is managed by the Champlain Water District (CWD). Raw water is pumped from Lake Champlain through a 28-inch diameter pipe that extends one-half mile out from shore. The water moves through a filtration process, coming in contact with water-quality instrumentation such as level, pressure, and flow transmitters, most of which are not date-sensitive. So, for starters, this instrumentation is not vulnerable to the Year 2000 problem, unless, of course, there is no electricity to power the pump.

Water moves through the Champlain Water District at an average rate of 10.6 million gallons a day (this figure is for the fiscal year that ended on June 30, 1998). The CWD system supplies twelve municipal water systems serving sixty-five thousand customers. A computer manufacturer is a major consumer, using four and a quarter million gallons of water a day, roughly 40 percent of CWD's entire output. CWD's storage capacity is 13.653 million gallons of treated water.

Three water mains leave the treatment plant carrying water to 70 square miles of Vermont, distributing it to sixteen water storage tanks, which range in size from 225,000 to 2.2 million gallons. Six booster pump stations are used to increase pressure, pushing water to the storage tanks, which are at higher elevations in Chittenden County. Once the water reaches the storage tanks, it is fed by gravity to the businesses and homes in the district, called, in water parlance, end users.

How vulnerable is the whole system to Y2K? We interviewed Paul Tice, CWD's Information and Engineering System Director. Early in 1997, Paul brought possible Y2K problems to the attention of the district. He had learned of the issue from computer trade publications and believed it was essential to assess CWD's vulnerabilities. Paul keeps a notebook, labeled "Y2K compliance," of correspondence related to the Year 2000 problem and its effect on CWD. Half the notebook is devoted to the physical plant and the movement of water from the plant to its destination. The other half is full of local area network information for billing and accounting. Paul expects to have three additional notebooks filled with similar information before the year 2000 arrives. It is clear that, even for a relatively small water district, assessing Y2K vulnerability can be a daunting problem.

Paul began the Y2K assessment with an on-site appraisal along with CWD's equipment vendor. Together they walked the plant "inch by inch." Whenever they arrived at an instrument installation, they recorded the location and equipment information. Although they have finished the initial inventory process, they are still collecting data from individual manufacturers to assess Y2K compliance of equipment that has been inventoried.

Paul told us that he was amazed by "the little things that are often overlooked. An instrument used to check water for the level of chlorine actually has a date-sensitive chip that needs to be investigated. People need to look past the surface."

Other vulnerabilities in the system include the programmable logic controllers (PLCs) at the pump stations. If not replaced, a PLC's internal clock may reset to 1980 just when the real clock has turned its hands to the year 2000, because 1980 seems to be a common default date for most of the embedded chips that Paul has evaluated. If this happens, the system could lock up or it could reset itself to the year 1980. At first glance, would it really matter if the embedded chip thought it was 1980? Unfortunately, yes. A 1980 date would bring faulty data to the main control system, and this misinformation might cause problems. For example, pumps may read that they are off when they actually are on. All the data coming in would have to be verified for accuracy, an impossible task. And this is only one example of vulnerability. Other potential problems lie in the twenty-eight metering sites (five with flow control), two pressure-reducing vaults to accommodate smaller distribution systems, and four check-valve vaults, which prevent backflow.

The Chaplain Water District decided to address the potential problems that lie within the water distribution system by installing a new piece of equipment: the Supervisory Control and Data Acquisition system, known in the trade as SCADA, which is Y2K-compliant and replaces the operation of all plant and field controllers. The system has the added advantage of standing alone, meaning it only communicates with field transmitters, eliminating the possibility of having the data or system corrupted by outside communication from a source that is not Y2K-compliant. SCADA brings all data back to one central location for review and control. Anything in the field that has some type of control, whether it's turning a pump on or off, controlling a valve, or initiating filter washing, can be done at a single workstation in the main plant with the double click of a mouse. More impressive and reassuring is the system's compliancy with respect to Y2K. CWD plans to complete the installation of SCADA by the end of 1998 and will use the following twelve months to assess any further vulnerabilities—within SCADA or independent of it.

Of course, power is CWD's biggest vulnerability. To ensure the plant's resilience, two lines run from Green Mountain Power (GMP), the local utility, to the plant, and another two lines run from GMP to the raw-water station. This redundancy came in handy in the spring of 1998 when a splice in one of the lines became corroded and needed replacing. The job took four hours and simply involved switching over to the backup line while the work went on, and switching back when it was over. Water service was not interrupted.

CWD currently relies on GMP, in concert with the Vermont Public Service Board, to complete similar Y2K investigations so that there will be an uninterrupted supply of power in the future. CWD is also investigating alternative power supplies that could be used if needed. The district does have a small generator fueled by natural gas that keeps the master SCADA station running in case of a power failure at the plant, which allows control of field equipment. This generator is turned on once a week for an hour as a maintenance measure. However, without power, water processing and distribution stops. Should the main plant lose power, CWD's general manager is considering renting a large generator (costing roughly $30,000) so the plant could be run at about one-third its normal volume. Additionally, gasoline-powered portable pumps are being considered as backups to the six pump stations that will be idle if power is disrupted. The water in the storage tanks would last only one day, or, if conservation measures were implemented quickly and industrial use was reduced, stretched to two days. This shows that there are still vulnerabilities in the system. To address them, once CWD receives Green Mountain Power's Y2K report, the district will implement whatever measures it must to ensure an uninterrupted supply of water to the sixty-five thousand people it serves.

If you are part of a municipal water system, it would be a good idea to ask those in charge about how water gets to your home. By asking questions about the strengths and vulnerabilities of the system, you may encourage local leaders to take action (if they are not already doing so). And you'll be able to relax if you discover that those in charge have studied the municipal water system with respect to Y2K and have made sure it is compliant.

How to Store Water

If your municipal water system seems vulnerable, or if you do not have a backup generator or hand pump for your well, then by all means store enough water for emergency needs. Plan on a minimum of 14 gallons of water per person for a two week emergency, or one gallon per day, which will only supply two quarts for drinking and two quarts for cleaning and bathing. Given normal water use, this is a very minimal amount. Remember to provide for your pets' needs as well.

Whatever storage method you choose, be sure to keep water away from harmful chemicals or products that have a nasty smell, as odors and toxic materials can penetrate your containers. A dark, cool location is best. Water needs to be purified before storing (see How to Purify Water on page 108). Here are some storage suggestions:

- 55-gallon drums: According to an Internet article written by Walton Feed, food-grade plastic (polyethylene) 55-gallon drums are ideal for bulk water storage. You can get them from food storage or local container companies listed in the Yellow Pages of your phone book. Make sure there is a spigot that is easy to reach.
- 5-gallon bottles: *Making the Best of Basics* recommends using 5-gallon containers of a plastic grade that meets the Department of Transportation (DOT) #34 standard, because water weighs eight pounds per gallon and anything bigger than five gallons is too hard to move around. Fifteen-gallon containers are also available and, if the emergency outlasts your water supply, you can haul these to a water source, such as a pond or stream, using a wheelbarrow or garden cart.
- Single-use packets: These 4.225-ounce metallized sachets of water are available from Aquacheck. Each case contains sixty packets with a five-year shelf life with water that has been purified, sterilized, and sealed in airtight pouches to prevent bacteria growth. Water packets withstand temperatures ranging from -40°F to 230°F, are easier to

transport than a large water bottle if you are forced to leave your home, are approved by the U.S. Coast Guard, and can be used as cold compresses. The major disadvantage is cost, which is $14.95 a case. In the continental U.S., you can order toll-free, 1–800–504–5580. Outside of the continental U.S. the number is 714–739–7755.

- A low-cost storage strategy is to fill well-rinsed, empty soda bottles. Milk jugs are not suitable because they are biodegradable and break down within six months.

If your stored supply runs low, consider other sources of water in your home. For example, the water heater typically holds between 15 and 40 gallons, which may be used for drinking or cooking. You'll need to open the drain faucet on the bottom of the heater; the water may need to be filtered to catch any sediment. If there is snow outside, collect, melt, and purify it for your use. Rain barrels or other containers are an excellent strategy for having extra water on hand at all times. Make sure they are clean, but, even if they are, purify the water you collect in them to be safe.

Harvesting Rainwater

A more elaborate storage solution is to create a rainwater harvesting system, for which you will probably need professional help. This system uses your roof, gutters, and downspouts to direct the water, a filtering system, a cistern to hold the water, and a distribution method to get the collected rainwater into the house. Here are some guidelines for a proper rainwater harvesting system:

- Any roofing material is acceptable if the water will not be used for drinking. If you have an asbestos roof, you cannot drink the water collected from it, and asphalt shingles contribute grit to the system, requiring a pre-filter before water reaches the cistern. The best roofing materials for collecting rainwater are metal, clay, or cement.
- Roof washers, which isolate and direct the first water to fall on the roof away from the cistern, while allowing the rest of the rainwater

to enter the gutters, downspouts, and cistern, are commercially available. Ten gallons of rainfall per thousand square feet of roof is an acceptable amount of water for washing. However, if you are collecting water for irrigation purposes only, you do not need a washer. A sand filter can be used to filter the water to reduce sediment buildup.

- A distribution system for the collected rainwater can use gravity if the cistern is placed higher than the water's destination. A pump, similar to a well pump, could be installed if necessary. However, to make your collection system resilient, you should also have a hand pump.
- Gutter materials should be a minimum of 26-gauge galvanized steel or 0.025-inch aluminum. The front of the gutter should be ½ inch lower than the back, and the slope should be a minimum of $\frac{1}{16}$ of an inch per foot. They should be fitted with a leaf screen to filter out contaminants.
- Downspouts should supply 1 square inch of downspout opening for every 100 square feet of roof area.
- The maximum run of gutter for one downspout is 50 feet.
- Cisterns can be located above or below ground. You should choose a size that will allow maximum rainwater collection for your area. Check with your local weather forecasters for average rainfall amounts in your locality. The best materials for cisterns are concrete, steel, ferro-cement, or fiberglass. When ordering a cistern, specify if it will be an above- or below-ground installation and if it will be used to store potable water. Cistern interiors should be smooth and clean and all joints should be sealed with nontoxic, waterproof materials. A cover is necessary to prevent insect breeding and algae growth.

Storing water may sound like a lot of work and extra expense. However, you can always use stored water for cooking and drinking after we settle into the new millennium and find that everything is okay. Even so, it is a good idea to have potable water in the event of an ice storm, flood, hurricane, tornado, or earthquake. If any of these events are possible where you live, hang on to this stored treasure just in case.

How to Purify Water

Since we generally use tap water for storage and cannot be sure it is free of bacteria, it has to be purified. Some studies indicate that bacteria-free water stored in clean opaque containers may last for several years. Other authorities suggest renewing your stored water every six months. In any case, storing water for long periods of time may affect its taste.

Four techniques are available to purify water. The easiest way is to bring water to a good rolling boil for ten minutes, so that it reaches 212°F/100°C. This is reasonably safe, inexpensive, and requires no special equipment. But it will take time and energy to boil enough water to satisfy the needs of a family.

A purifying method favored by some experts involves a stabilized oxygen product called Ion, made by Arloxy of America, which is very effective at killing bacteria without harmful side effects. In fact, it has medicinal properties; for example, it makes bug bites stop itching instantly. Use twenty drops per gallon of water for long-term storage. It kills giardia, cholera, dysentery, and other harmful bacteria in two and one-half minutes. A 2-ounce bottle sells for $14.95 and purifies 63 gallons of water. Ion is available from Walton Feed, 135 North 10th, PO Box 307, Montpelier, ID 83254; 800-269-8563; fax 208-847-0467; Web site http://waltonfeed.com/ion4.html.

Traditionally, a 2 percent tincture of iodine has been used as a water purifier. Twelve drops purifies one gallon of water. However, pregnant women and people with thyroid problems should not drink iodized water, and it should be reserved for emergency use only.

Finally, ordinary chlorine bleach will purify water. Look for household bleach that contains a 5.25 percent solution of sodium hypochlorite without soap additives or phosphates. Use ⅛ teaspoon, or about five to eight drops, per gallon of water.

WATER FILTERS

Filters are another way to clean water. They are effective against a broad spectrum of contaminants. If you decide to invest in a filtering system, make sure the filtration system you choose is certified by the National Safety Foundation (NSF). You can select a ceramic filter, which will cost about $190 to $200, or a mechanical system. The mechanical systems fit either on top of a kitchen counter ($158), or under the counter for between $266 and $400. Reverse osmosis filters are much costlier, running $532 for a counter-top model and about $600 for an under-the-counter model. Portable water filters are also available if that is a need in your home. If your water supply is not pressure-fed, you can choose a gravity filter, which can produce as much as ten gallons of drinking water a day. All these filters are available from the Ace Pump Corporation, 57 West 21st Street, New York, NY 10010; 888-242-4500; email: sales@acepump.com.

How to Heat Water

Although you can live without hot water, living with it makes life a lot easier. Most water is heated either with a free-standing hot water tank powered by electricity or gas, or a tank or tankless hot water heat exchanger connected to the furnace. A hot water tank is obviously dependent on electricity if that is the source of its power, but the hot water heat exchanger is too because it needs electricity to circulate the hot water and to ignite the furnace.

In a power failure, heat water either on your wood stove or any other alternative stove. You can purchase tankless hot water heaters that do not require electricity to heat or deliver hot water. These are called instantaneous heaters and are independent of your home furnace. They cost between $640 to $700, a good alternative to a conventional hot water heater.

Sanitation

If you depend upon a municipal sanitation system, you can't do much beyond asking the mayor or town manager what is being done to prevent Y2K breakdowns in sanitation services. If you are not satisfied that enough is being done, attend meetings of the Planning Commission or the Select board, or write letters to the local newspapers and television stations. If garbage removal is not a municipal service where you live, you should ask the same questions of the company that comes to get your recyclables and trash.

Since one of us and our researcher, Karen Moore, live in Shelburne, Vermont (population 6,500), Karen spent an hour talking with the town manager about Shelburne's sanitation system. Not only was he happy to talk with us, he was helpful in correcting some of our Y2K worries and frank about what is resilient in the town and what needs to be studied further and improved.

Under normal circumstances, when we flush our toilets, take a shower, or wash the dishes, the waste is gravity-fed to sixteen lift stations throughout Shelburne. From these stations, the waste, which includes everything, liquid and solid, that goes down a drain in our homes, is pumped either to another lift station or directly to the wastewater treatment facility. The lift stations are located at low points, in some cases under bridges that cross rivers and near marshy areas, to allow gravity to do its job and collect the waste. The pumping, of course, requires electricity, as does the waste treatment facility.

In preparation for possible power outages, Shelburne is installing a diesel-powered generator at the lift station with the heaviest flow. (Some stations with very light flow pump for only ten minutes a day.) In addition, the town has a mobile generator that can be moved from one lift station to another. These generators mean that our town should be able to provide adequate sanitation services during any kind of a power outage, whether caused by storms or Y2K.

As a further backup, Shelburne has a tank truck that can visit the lift stations, pump the waste out manually, and take it to the waste facility for treatment. During a prolonged power outage, if the one tank truck is not sufficient to keep up with the waste, the town has a contingency plan to contract with waste disposal businesses to transport wastewater from lift stations to the treatment facility. During the ice storm of January 1998, Shelburne made arrangements with independent sources for five tank trucks. Shelburne's truck plus the additional trucks ran for two days until power was restored. To alleviate strain on the lift stations and trucks, the town used the local radio stations to request residents to conserve water use.

However, if the Y2K bug causes disruptions in the gasoline supply, how long could these tank trucks operate? And if there is enough gasoline, would the tank trunks be able to keep up with the demand of all the towns around them?

The town manager commented that, ideally, a wastewater disposal system would not have lift stations, and some towns do not; it depends on the topography of the area coupled with the location of the wastewater treatment facility. The State of Vermont has added a level of resilience to new lift stations, requiring them to have a four-hour storage capacity.

In the event that none of the contingency plans work, Shelburne's residents would still be able to flush toilets (if they had water), and the waste would be gravity-fed to the lift stations. Here it would collect, and, during a prolonged outage, it would eventually back up in a spiderweb of underground pipes. The waste would then find its way into homes and manholes, or it could overflow at the lift stations onto the land, contaminating our surface waterways and, ultimately, our groundwater.

It was reassuring to learn that as long as the waste can be pumped or trucked to the treatment facility it can be processed. That facility has two emergency power generators. The first is a diesel generator with a 500-gallon fuel reserve. On the day we called, the tank was half full with fourteen-year-old fuel, a supply that would last about three days. There is also a propane generator with a 1,000-gallon capacity. The generators are test-run once a week for maintenance purposes.

Some questions still remain: Can the tanks be kept topped off, thus extending the town's resiliency at minimal cost? Should additional fuel reserves be considered? How often does the fuel need to be rotated and renewed, and how can this be accomplished?

By checking into your local town's situation, and asking questions about the process of collecting and treating wastewater, the strengths and vulnerabilities of the system can be assessed, and your community's leaders can be encouraged to take action. In our community, the town manager believes the fuel supply and fuel reserves to be the most vulnerable part of the system. The emergency backup plans depend upon gasoline, propane, and diesel fuel, which, in a worst-case scenario, may not be readily available. Shelburne town officials are analyzing the status of fuel supplies and the capacity of fuel reserve tanks to see if additional resilience can be developed.

Your town can also begin an information campaign, alerting residents through local newspapers and TV and radio stations about how wastewater is collected and about the sanitation risks involved in a prolonged power outage. People can be urged to limit water use and to flush only solid wastes during a power outage. To further reduce the demand on the wastewater treatment facility, town residents can be encouraged to compost appropriate kitchen waste instead of using the garbage disposal in their sink. As an added benefit, you'll have wonderful organic compost for the vegetables and flowers you are growing.

As we pointed out earlier, if you have a well with an electric pump, it obviously will not work during a power outage. Thus you may be without water for washing or flushing the toilet. During the 1998 ice storm, Bev was blessed with a neighbor with a leaky basement, whose sump pump had gone out with the electricity. Everyone on the block volunteered with buckets to bail out the basement, and then carried the water home to flush the toilets. A very time-consuming and labor-intensive solution, but it worked. However, since we cannot all depend on neighbors with leaky basements, a small backup generator with plenty of stored fuel would be a resilient solution (see the section on generators in chapter 4). A hand pump may also be useful.

Disposing of Garbage and Waste

If there are disruptions in water or sanitation service, here are some steps you can take to get through the rough times with minimum discomfort:

Have adequate supplies on hand: Make certain you have an adequate supply of stored water, toilet paper, soaps, toothpaste and brushes, deodorant, nonelectric razors, sanitary pads or tampons, large plastic garbage bags, household cleaners, and bleach. If you have a baby, be certain that you have baby powder and cream, baby wipes, disposable diapers, and anything else you may need. Remember your pets—you may need to store extra kitty litter, for example.

Reduce waste: Try to reduce waste by preparing only the amount of food your family can consume at each meal, wearing the same clothes as long as you can (since your ability to wash them will be limited until the water is restored), and recycling everything you can for a second use.

Separate the garbage: Store recyclables as you normally do. If you have too many, put them in large plastic bags. See-through bags would be useful, or use masking tape to note their contents. Store them outside, preferably in a garage or shed. If you have been eating out of cans, first scour the cans with sand or snow to clean them, or use a damp paper towel where water is limited. The more you can eventually recycle, the less trash will go to the landfill.

Put all non-food and non-recyclable garbage together in large heavy plastic bags. Store them outside in a garage or shed. Eventually someone will come for them or you will be able to take them to the landfill.

You can create a primitive compost heap by piling vegetable, fruit, and grain scraps in a mound away from the house. Do not include any dairy products, fat, bones, or meat products, as these will attract animals. Meat scraps and other food refuse can first be put in heavy plastic bags and then into animal-proof garbage containers. If it is cold enough outside, the contents will freeze, adding another level of safety.

Dispose of human waste: If you find yourself without water and cannot flush the toilet, urinate outside, or use a bucket and bury the contents far away from the house, as our ancestors did with their slops before indoor plumbing came along. You could build an outhouse, but that's probably a pretty extreme solution for the average emergency, which is usually over within a week or two. More practically, you can line the toilet with a large plastic bag before using it, tie the bag, and transport it in a bucket to store it somewhere far from the house until the emergency is over, or until you can bury the contents.

Consider installing a composting toilet: A composting toilet is a large, warm, externally vented container with a variety of aerobic microbes that break down waste materials into a dry, fluffy, odorless compost that your lawn and flower garden will love. Water is evaporated by the warm air-flow, helped along by a cup of peat moss added daily. Composting toilets work best at a temperature of 70°F or warmer. A variety of models are available. Some are complete units installed in the bathroom; other designs put the toilet in the bathroom and connect it to a composting chamber outside the bathroom. Since these toilets must be well ventilated by fans, they are designed to work with regular electricity or generators. Their major drawback is cost, which runs from $950 to $1,500 on average, though some Cadillac models go as high as $4,500. For more information on composting toilets, take a look at the *Solar Living Source-book* from Real Goods.

For those who don't want to invest this kind of money, spend $19.95 on *The Humanure Handbook*, a complete guide to composting human ex-crement the low-tech, inexpensive way. Another book on the same sub-ject is *The Toilet Papers*, a history of how people have dealt with human waste over the centuries, which reviews available alternatives, such as dry toilets, compost privies, and graywater systems. All three books are avail-able by calling 1-800-762-7325.

While the most resilient home will have its own well, with a backup generator to pump water (or a hand pump), even those people on a municipal supply can pay attention to water storage and the san-itary disposal of wastes and make their homes safe and comfortable during an emergency.

CHAPTER 8

HEALTH

> But it's entirely possible that millennium conversion
> could put the health care industry into intensive care.
>
> SENATOR CHRISTOPHER DODD,
> *testifying before the U. S. Senate Special Committee*
> *on the Year 2000 Technology Problem, July 23, 1998*

SINCE THE Y2K BUG is a disease limited to computer software and embedded processors, how can it affect your health?

Nothing is harder on your health than uncertainty—and Y2K represents uncertainty to the tenth power. Even the experts cannot agree whether the problems will be major or minor. There is a vast difference between occasional disruptions and a complete breakdown of infrastructure—the two ends of the probability scale. Since we can only guess at the virulence of the Y2K problem, a wait-and-see approach could add to your stress.

What happens once January 1, 2000 arrives? The Y2K bug is probably not going to be a twenty-four-hour flu. There is no consensus about how long-lasting its effects may be. Some predict up to a year of intermittent disruptions of essential services.

Consider how dependent your well-being is on supplies from outside sources and the infrastructure that makes services possible. You turn on the tap expecting clean water, adjust the thermostat to make your home comfortable, flick on the light switch when it is dark, order prescription medicines on the telephone (which you expect the drug-store will have in stock), visit the grocery store to buy food for dinner. The absence of power, phone service, medicine, or food presents enormous problems, which are likely to create a lot of stress on you and your family.

A proactive approach can help in two ways. First, it can help channel your anxiety about the Y2K bug into useful action. Second, preparing for your health needs now can mean a more resilient home if and when services are disrupted.

How to Deal with Y2K Stress

Medical science has increasingly demonstrated that many of the diseases we suffer from may start with mental or emotional stress, which contributes to the weakening of the immune system. Researchers have also pointed out the connection between prayer and healing. It is clear that the body is not compartmentalized but is one unit: stress in one area affects another area. In other words, a happy heart and mind can have profoundly beneficial effects on the body, and an unhappy pair can cause no end of physical damage. So when we think of stress, we think of the interrelatedness between the body, mind, and spirit.

Of course, stress also has an important function because, as danger approaches, the fight-or-flight reflex takes over, allowing animals and people to become combative or run away to escape danger. When the odds seem overwhelming, freezing and hiding may be the best solution. Each to their own: the elephant attacks, the fox runs from the hounds, and the mouse halts, hoping its stillness and dull color will allow it to escape the hawk's notice. But we needn't get to the fight-or-flight point. We are able to recognize intellectually the problem represented by Y2K, consider alternatives, and choose to act in a useful way.

While stress has its positive aspects, unremitting stress can take a toll on the immune system and its ability to fight disease. Until you have lived for a week or two without power and/or water, it may be difficult to imagine how stressful it can be. Of course it is not as bad as something like losing a home to flood waters (with or without flood insurance), but it can be significant and exhausting.

Thus, the first step to safeguard your health during a Y2K emergency is to prepare your home as has been suggested in previous chapters. Then you can decide how to minimize stress if and when the power grid goes down or the phones fail. Here are some suggestions:

1. Maintain a routine. If you can't get to work or other activities, it may be tempting to stay in bed all day or sit curled up in a blanket reading, but don't do it. Of course if you have children, particularly if they are not in school, this passive behavior will not be an option. Whatever your situation, establish and maintain a routine, because this will help you feel in control of your life, and will alleviate some stress. Prepare and eat regular meals, set aside a time for exercise, tidy the house, plan future projects, visit the neighbors, listen to music, go for a walk, pursue a hobby, write in a diary. Bev knows of one family who, during a prolonged power outage, were so appalled at the amount of time they customarily spent watching TV, and were so delighted with the projects and games they devised for their children during the blackout, that they canceled their cable service.

If you have children, and they can't get to school, spend part of the day teaching them at home. This certainly would be a great time for a unit about electricity. When they tire of their own games, you can invite them to join in your exercise routine, work with you in the house, visit the neighbors, and play games together. As difficult as disruptions in power can be, they can provide a chance for real family togetherness.

2. Eat three healthy meals and drink plenty of water. Some of us respond to stress by not eating, others by overeating. Neither is good for your health. Even though your food supply may be limited to canned foods that do not have to be cooked, and even if they are not the tastiest morsels you have ever consumed, it is important to keep to a regular schedule of three meals a day.

Make sure you have at least one month's supply of supplements and vitamins (although three months would be better), as you may need these to maintain an adequate nutritional intake. And it is absolutely essential, so we don't mind repeating it, to have enough bottled water—one or two gallons a day for each person in your home.

Remember that if you don't have adequate nutrition your immune system may not function at full speed. You don't want to add illness to an already compromised situation of shortages.

3. Exercise: This could prove to be one of the hidden benefits of Y2K. Since it is wise to check with your doctor before beginning any exercise program, do it now. And, having checked, try to find the incentive and discipline to begin. This is another way to prepare our bodies for Y2K. Exercise is not only essential to the proper functioning of our bodies, it is a way to channel our stress before, during, and after Y2K.

Your doctor may suggest that you vary your exercise routine to include aerobic exercise. This form of exercise includes walking, dancing, running, biking, or using an exercise tape, though that may not be available if your TV and VCR stop working when the power fails. Strength exercise uses resistance or weights, which could be something as simple as holding unopened soup cans in your hands while you do some prescribed arm exercises, or doing exercises with two-, three-, or five-pound weights, which you can buy at any sporting goods store. Whatever routine your doctor recommends, remember to start at a comfortable level, and increase the amount of exercise slowly as your fitness develops.

4. Keep your environment organized. As we all know, living in a messy house can be stressful in and of itself. The more control you feel you have over your situation, the less stress you will feel. When you finish an activity, put away the things you used. As for young kids, it's amazing how organized toys and open floor space can stimulate their imaginative play.

5. Talk about the situation, especially to your children. Your attitude, the way you react to any emergency, can be your most important ally, or your most threatening enemy. You may find it useful to set aside a regular time for discussing what is happening, the news you've heard on your battery-operated radio, and how long the disruptions may last. Remember to be a support for your child; don't ask your child to support you. Such a reversal of roles could be damaging to children already under great stress.

Very young children will usually feel safe as long as they are with you and their needs are adequately met. However, if you are very upset, they will sense it and may act out their feelings of fear and insecurity. Try to be patient and understanding if they start acting out. Reassure them that what is happening is only a phase that will be over at some point, and that you will take care of them—this reassurance can go a long way toward calming them down.

Older children may need help naming or expressing their concerns. Adult-supervised play with a dollhouse, or drawing pictures of a Y2K-resilient home, may help them express and deal with their anxieties.

You may also be dealing with unexpected emotions. Despite your Y2K preparations, you may find yourself haunted by anxiety, fears of the unknown, and even feelings of abandonment. Such feelings are a necessary part of the human condition—we really do not have as much control over life as a century of advances in science and medicine have led us to believe. Remember to follow the suggestions given above: Maintain a routine; eat and drink properly; exercise; and talk to others. Also, some people find it useful to deal with these emotions through the disciplines of their faith—prayer, meditation, music, or keeping a journal.

However, if these feelings appear to be more than you can handle on your own, and talking to others as recommended does not help, make every effort to visit with a health professional. (See below for suggestions about emergency health care.)

6. Enjoy community support. One way to alleviate your own stress is to focus on other people. Make sure your neighbors are okay, particularly elderly people who live alone. This will not only help your neighbors, it will teach your children about compassion. If necessary, invite your elderly neighbor or anyone else who needs help or comfort to visit or even live temporarily in your Y2K-resilient home.

One of the benefits of our ice storm was how some neighborhoods coalesced and helped each other. Bev's block even had a party on what turned out to be the final night of the emergency. Neighbors brought food and everyone ate up all the freezer contents that had defrosted because, ironically, 30°F was not cold enough to keep food frozen, even though it was cold enough to create all that ice. It was a gala event, and everyone felt pretty good because rumor had it that the power would be restored the following day.

Try to develop community rapport before Y2K. Then, if services are disrupted, it will be natural for the community to pull together and help one another. (See chapter 10 for more on community.)

How to Handle Chronic Health Conditions

If you or any member of your family, including young children, take regular over-the-counter or prescription medication, make sure you have a minimum of one month's supply in reserve, though three months would be better. If your medication is expensive, it will take some financial planning and saving to set aside enough money for your drug cache.

For prescription drugs, this also means explaining to your doctor, who may be loathe to give repeat prescriptions, about the possible shortages that may occur due to delivery breakdowns or the temporary closing of manufacturing plants or drugstores because of assorted computer malfunctions. The object, however you achieve it, is to make sure your physician prescribes enough medication for the anticipated time period that supplies may not be available.

The timing of supply disruptions is uncertain. Trouble may wait to occur in January 2000, or there might be delivery problems during 1999, because of expiration dates that extend beyond the year 2000. There have been reports of computers refusing delivery of foods with expiration dates in the year 2000 and the same problem may affect the drug industry. Or there may be no disruptions at all.

Don't make medical appointments close to the New Year. If you have chronic health needs that require electrical equipment, arrange for a backup generator. When in doubt, check with your doctor.

How to Handle Emergency Health Care

You can avoid some emergencies by planning ahead. For example, to be on the safe side, try to avoid having a baby between, say, December 1999 and March 2000. Alternately, you may want to check with your doctor or midwife about emergency backup plans.

Make sure you see your dentist regularly in 1999 and have any required work done; you don't want to come down with a toothache when you can't reach your dentist. If you suffer from a condition that can be helped by surgery, consider having elective surgery now.

It would also be wise to sharpen your first-aid skills. Most communities give courses in basic first aid, including cardiopulmonary resuscitation (CPR), and there is no better time than now to have some member of your family take these courses. Contact your local Red Cross office or rescue squad to find out when they plan to give such courses. Learn how to stock a first-aid kit properly, and make sure yours has everything in it you may need. The kit should include bandages and adhesive strips, disinfectants, antibiotic cream, aspirin and Tylenol, splints and slings, antihistamines, anti-itch creams, nose drops, cough drops, and cough medicine.

To prepare for a phone outage, find out your doctor's office hours so you can simply arrive there if you have a problem. In a large metropolitan area, you can go directly to the hospital emergency room. If you live in a small town with a volunteer rescue squad, find out what plans they are making to give service in case of a phone or electricity blackout. If they do not intend to have staff at the rescue garage, get a schedule of crew chiefs, with their duty times and addresses, so that you can go to their houses if necessary.

However, this advice is only good if you can use your car. During the great ice storm of January 1998, Bev had a hard time disconnecting the garage door from its motor. After she managed it, she could not open the heavy garage door manually. She called her neighbor and together, like Atlas, they lifted it up. So make sure that the control that separates the door from the electric motor is working properly and that you can lift the door by hand, so that your car doesn't stay trapped in your garage. And be sure that your car has a full tank of gas at all times as we approach the millennium.

If you are too ill to use the car, you will need to have a driver. Arrange emergency backup with a neighbor.

Staying Healthy in Extreme Cold

Some individuals, especially young children and the elderly, may suffer from hypothermia even in a home that is warm enough to be comfortable for others. Since the Y2K problems are likely to surface in January, a good part of the country may be dealing with winter weather. Here are some hints for surviving the cold:

Hypothermia means that the body temperature has fallen below 95°F. The symptoms are unmistakable—slurred or slow speech; incoherence, memory loss, and disorientation; uncontrollable shivering; repeated stumbling; drowsiness and apparent exhaustion. If someone has these symptoms, take her temperature and if it is below 95°, seek immediate medical help.

If medical help is not available, start warming the trunk of the body first by getting the person into dry clothes, wrap her in a warm blanket covering the head and neck, and, if necessary, use your own body heat to warm her. Don't give hot beverages, alcohol, or drugs; warm broth is best. Do not warm extremities before the body trunk because this will drive the cold blood toward the heart and can produce heart failure.

Frostbite occurs after exposure of the skin to extreme cold. Fingers, toes, the nose, and earlobes are most often affected, but any exposed skin can be frostbitten, and damage can be permanent. The symptoms are loss of feeling in the affected area and white or pale skin color. Frostbite is unlikely to occur inside a resilient home, but staying outdoors too long without adequate clothing may result in frostbite. Seek medical help at once for anyone afflicted with frostbite but, if it is not available, slowly re-warm the affected areas. Remember that if the victim has hypothermia as well, warm the body trunk first as described above.

In general, wear loose-fitting, lightweight, warm clothing in several layers, because the air trapped between the layers provides insulation. This gives you a lot of flexibility—if you get too warm you can remove a layer or two so that you don't perspire, which can make your clothing damp and your body chilled in cold surroundings. Be sure your outdoor clothing is tightly woven and water repellent, and always wear a hat or hood outside, because a good percentage of your body heat is lost through a bare head. Use a scarf to cover your mouth to protect your lungs. Mittens that are snug at the wrist keep your hands warmer than gloves, which can allow your fingers to cool quickly. Stay as dry as possible, but if your clothes do get wet, change them. Do not stay outside for too long at any one time to avoid hypothermia and frostbite.

Staying Healthy in Extreme Heat

Young children and the elderly are sensitive to extreme heat. Since there is no consensus on when Y2K disruptions may occur, and some likelihood that power failures may occur sporadically throughout the year 2000, you should try to avoid heat illness during an infrastructure breakdown by staying out of the hot sun, wearing as little and as light clothing as possible, and knowing what to do in heat emergencies. Heat illness comes in three forms:

Heat cramps, the least serious of the heat illnesses, usually affect the leg muscles after strenuous exercise, but have been known to afflict factory workers as well. Dehydration and electrolyte imbalance may be the cause. To treat heat cramps, the person should move to a cooler area if possible, sit or lie down until the cramps subside, and drink water or a balanced electrolyte solution. Do not give salt tablets or salty fluids, as these folks have adequate electrolytes in their systems, they are just not well distributed.

Heat exhaustion, also known as heat prostration or heat collapse, is the most common heat problem. It occurs when the body loses too much fluid. Sweating is only an effective cooling mechanism if the sweat can evaporate from the body. Therefore, do not wear excess clothing when in the hot sun or in humid environments. Symptoms include a gray face, cold and clammy skin, and possible dizziness, weakness, and nausea. Some people may faint from heat exhaustion. To treat a person with these symptoms, remove tight and excessive layers of clothing, have him lie down, and if the person is fully alert give up to a liter of water to drink. (If not alert do not force water because it could be aspirated into the lungs, causing more serious problems.) Usually the symptoms subside after 30 minutes but if they do not, and particularly if the level of awareness or consciousness drops, call an ambulance or take the person to the nearest hospital emergency room.

Heatstroke is the most serious of these conditions, since it will kill a victim if not treated promptly. Heatstroke occurs during strenuous physical activity, particularly in a closed, poorly ventilated, humid environment. It is also a frequent problem during heat waves, particularly for the elderly, and children have been known to die after being left alone in a locked car on a hot summer day. Symptoms include a hot, dry, flushed skin, increased body temperature, reduced level of consciousness, weak pulse, and lowered blood pressure.

This is a real medical emergency. Call an ambulance at once. The patient's body must be cooled by any means available to avoid death. The first step is to remove the person from the hot environment if possible; if air conditioning is available, it should be set on high. Remove all clothing, put wet towels or sheets on the body, and aim a fan at the patient. Inform the hospital in advance about the problem so that they can have an ice bath ready for immediate use.

All this advice sounds serious, perhaps scary, but being prepared is the best armor you can have to stay healthy during an emergency.

CHAPTER 9

MONEY, TRANSPORTATION, AND COMMUNICATION

> From your personal computer, to the massive computer systems
> that run our government, our power grids, telecommunications,
> financial markets, and defense systems, the Year 2000 problem
> has the potential to be devastating.
>
> SENATOR PATRICK LEAHY,
> *News conference, December 29, 1998*

 IN CASE THIS IS THE ONLY BOOK YOU READ
about Y2K, this chapter covers other areas of your life that
may be affected by the millennium bug, including banking
and financial services, the home office, home appliances,
and, very briefly, transportation and communication. It at-
tempts to answer the following questions: Will your home
appliances work on January 1, 2000? Can you keep the computers in your
home office going if the power grid goes down? Will your broker know
what securities you own? Will the banks function? And will you be able to
get to work however you commute—by car, bus, or train?

Financial Services

The greatest danger here is panic. It is important to remember that the
best way to create a banking emergency is to take all your money out of
the bank because, if everyone does that, the banks will not be able to
function. And there is no reason to do this. The banks are not likely to
run out of money, because the government is printing an extra fifty billion dollars and will print more if needed. Remember that the only thing
that can cause a financial panic is your response to a perceived problem.

It may be a good idea, however, to have some extra cash on hand over the New Year's weekend of 1999-2000 in case the ATM machines balk at the new millennium, but that is as far as we would advise you to go.

You should call your bank and find out if their computers are Y2K-compliant, and, if not, whether they are working on the problem and expect to fix their software before the end of 1999. It may comfort you to know that during a year-long banking strike in Ireland twenty years ago, life went on pretty much as usual. Using an original solution, checks became currency. It worked like this. If Mr. Flynn owed his plumber, Mr. O'Brien, $100, he wrote a check for that amount. Mr. O'Brien endorsed the check and used it to pay for new tools he needed. The hardware store from which he bought the tools endorsed the check again and used it to pay its supplier. And so it went: Checks with long lists of endorsements made the rounds instead of cash. No one panicked and everyone survived nicely. We're sure that Americans will be just as inventive as the Irish if they need to devise new financial survival techniques because of the millennium bug.

You should make sure you have hard copies of your financial records and of the stocks and bonds that you own. Ask your broker the same questions you asked the bank personnel. Find out what the company is doing about Y2K and whether it expects to achieve compliance before the deadline. It is encouraging to note that Wall Street ran a test during the summer of 1998, moving the date ahead to January 3, 2000, the first Monday of the new millennium, and found that computers handled the transition without a problem. As a whole, the financial services industry seems to be ahead of other sectors in dealing with the Year 2000 situation.

For example, one financial company started preparing for the changeover in 1996 by hiring eighty-five seasoned computer experts, plus outside consultants as needed, to identify and eliminate computer programming problems related to the Year 2000. A full-time program manager has been keeping track of the work and reports to the company's managing director of information technology. The company also created a Year 2000 advisory committee, composed of senior information technology staff and a representative from each major internal business group, which has been meeting weekly to track progress. The entire Y2K team has been working with the company's clients, business partners, and providers to assess the Y2K risks that outside computers interacting with their system may present, and it is checking the compliance schedules of all providers and partners. The team is preparing contingency plans to use if any of those outside systems are not ready by 2000. As a result of all their efforts, this major financial company expects to have fully tested its computers and to be ready for business without interruption when the millennium dawns.

The Home Office

More and more of us work at home. Our office computers not only store business and financial data but we also use them to write reports and business correspondence. All personal computers (PCs) have a calendar function; that is, when you turn the computer on, it tells you the date and time using its real time clock chip and its start-up software. Thus it is essential to contact the manufacturer of your computer to find out if it can read the year 2000 date correctly. Many manufacturers have toll-free telephone numbers and Web sites to answer your Y2K questions and quite a few provide free software upgrades so that older computers can read the date correctly. New start-up chips are available for older PCs, which you can hire a professional to install if you are not comfortable doing it yourself.

The computer's components—its modem, monitor, sound card, and graphics card—and the peripheral equipment, such as backup drives, may also contain embedded chips, but they may not use a calendar function. Nevertheless, it is a good idea to ask the manufacturer about their Y2K status.

As far as software goes, many of the programs we buy off the shelf are date sensitive because they process, store, and display dates. Date-sensitive software includes operating systems, such as DOS, OS/2, Windows, and Macintosh; databases and spreadsheets; accounting, financial, and tax software; project manager programs; utilities, such as file managers, personal information managers, un-installers, backup programs, and anti-virus software; and fax, e-mail, and other communication programs.

Most new operating systems should be able to handle the Year 2000 changeover, but you may need to download and install a software upgrade for some of them. Microsoft announced in late 1998 that it found two Y2K errors in its Windows 98; this goes to show the extent of the "bug." The best way to find out if you need an upgrade is to check the Web sites of your operating system or call the manufacturer's toll-free number. Apple Computer has said that the Macintosh operating system will not have any Y2K problems.

Scanners, copiers, and printers contain embedded chips but do not usually have calendar functions and should not have Y2K problems. Fax machines do have calendar functions. Manufacturers say that current models will not catch the millennium bug and older models will function, but they may stamp an incorrect date on incoming and outgoing faxes. Again, the manufacturer of all of these items will be able to tell you the score on the machines you own. Another source of help is the Federal Trade Commission (Washington, DC 20580; 202-FTC-HELP); it has brochures available on Y2K issues, which you can obtain by writing or calling them.

All in all, a few Web site visits or phone calls to technical support should allow your home office to function without problems after January 1, 2000. In addition, you may want to consider a UPS (Uninterrupted Power Supply) device for your home or office. These are designed to protect electronic equipment from surges, blackouts, brownouts, and spikes in electricity as well as lightning. The protection is in two parts: First, the UPS acts as a surge protector; and second, if the power goes down or the quality of power is degraded, you have time to power down the computer and turn it off without the loss of data. This can be accomplished because there is a small battery in the UPS. Some models allow as much as 10 or 15 minutes to close your computer.

"If it has a memory, it should be protected," says Jeff Wheeler at PC and Mac Connection. UPS devices range in price from $89 to over $500. The price range depends on many things including the battery capacity, run time, watts, the number of outlets it has, and how it's mounted. Most home needs, including those in home offices, will require the lower-priced models. To determine which model will best suit your needs, visit the Web site for American Power Conversion (www.sizing.apcc.com), and work through their Q & As. You'll end up with a recommendation specific to your needs.

These devices can last for years and years. Jeff Wheeler has been using the same UPS in his home office for ten to twelve years. The life of a UPS is related to the number of cycles the battery is exposed to. In some cases, batteries can be replaced and in other cases it makes sense to replace the device when the time comes. Additional precautions, if you haven't taken them already, include protecting other items in your home such as your VCR, TV, stereo, printer, monitor, and other appliances with surge protectors.

Home Appliances

Most homes have large and small appliances containing microchips— heating and cooling equipment, home entertainment audio/video products, photographic gear, calculators, wristwatches, electronic organizers, thermostats, and security systems. The good news is that many products that use the time of the day and/or the day of the week, such as programmable microwave ovens and coffeemakers, will probably not present a problem. Refrigerators, heating, and cooling equipment may have chips that keep track of cycles rather than dates and are unlikely to malfunction. Because few of these products use the month/date/year calendar function that is so central to computers, they will most likely enter the new millennium in fine working order. It is comforting to know, for example, that the Gas Appliance Manufacturers Association reports that furnaces, boilers, water heaters, and related products will not shut down as we enter 2000.

However, in some VCR models, particularly those manufactured before 1988, the time shift function that enables you to record future events may not work, but you will still be able to watch videotapes and tape TV programs. Some VCRs may allow you to reset the year to 2000 manually. In some camcorders, again those sold before 1988, the only problem will be an incorrect date display; everything else should work just fine. If you have a monitored security system whose calendar function is Y2K-compliant, check with the company to find out if their internal systems are also compliant. Do it now so you will not be locked into a contract with a monitoring company that has a problem after January 1, 2000. The FTC also has information on consumer electronic products, which you can obtain by using the address and phone number given above.

Transportation

New Year's Eve, 1999, may mean a great many things to different people, but there seems to be agreement on one particular piece of good news—your car will work. So will the buses. As far as commuter trains and city subways go, the best advice we can give is to check with the management of the local transportation companies to find out if they are Y2K-compliant, or if they expect equipment slowdowns or shutdowns. If you have an automatic garage door opener, it will not work if the electricity goes off, so make sure you know how to operate it manually. And fill your car or cars up with gas before January 1, just in case the local gas stations have not received deliveries, or the embedded chips in the pumps have turned themselves off. Of course, the real solution to any transportation problem is to live closer to where you work so that you can walk or bike back and forth. If Y2K transportation problems do crop up, that may be the wake-up call to rearrange your life and reduce the use of your car.

There is less optimism about the air traffic control system. It has been plagued with problems for years, with outmoded computers and new computer systems that do not work properly. One estimate is that a 30 percent cut in the number of flights may occur as the year 2000 dawns, and many experts are advising people not to travel over the New Year's weekend.

Communication

If the first thing you do in the morning is turn on the radio or TV for news, be sure to get a windup radio so that you can stay in touch with the world. Real Goods and Gardener's Supply sell windup radios; one windup gives you sixty minutes of listening. This is an Earth-friendly solution to staying in touch because it doesn't need batteries to run it.

If you are concerned about telephone service, check with your local phone company about their status regarding Y2K. An encouraging note: we had phone service all during the 1998 ice storm.

CHAPTER 10

COMMUNITY

> The National Association of Counties has just completed a survey . . . published just last week [showing] that roughly 50 percent of county governments . . . do not have a comprehensive Y2K readiness plan.
>
> JANET ABRAMS,
> *Executive Director of the President's Council on Year 2000*
> *Conversion, USIA Conference, December 17, 1998*

> The midst of a disaster is the poorest possible time to establish new relationships.
>
> ELIZABETH DOLE,
> *President of the Red Cross, Quoted in*
> *"Managing the Crisis You Tried to Prevent,"*
> Harvard Business Review, *Nov/Dec, 1995*

 WHICH COMES FIRST, A RESILIENT HOME or a Y2K-prepared community? Unless you live a very isolated life, it is hard to imagine one without the other. The first and most important task is to attend to your own home and meet its critical needs. Your home is probably the biggest investment and asset in your life. It cradles and frames your existence as a productive and participating member of the community in which you live, and to have it capable of functioning even when essential services have become unavailable is crucial.

Having provided for your family's needs, you can turn your attention to the community. The active, aware, and prepared community is the ideal complement to your resilient home. Not only does it double your own security, but you will have the satisfaction of being part of a larger effort as well. In the long run, we improve public welfare when communities learn once again to rely on local resources and take care of themselves.

For most of us, there are two aspects to community. One is your immediate neighborhood and, more personally, the street where you live. The second is the broader municipal district—city, town, or village—with all its various departments, such as those concerned with taxes, zoning, planning, and essential services.

The Neighborhood

Beverly tells this story about community: I live in a friendly neighborhood, where a block party in 1994 started a whole new feeling on our street. It came about like this: One day when I was shopping at our village market, I bumped into Alison James, a writer who lives nearby with her husband and two children. I know Alison pretty well because we belong to some of the same writers' organizations and talk about professional problems frequently. It was May and Vermont smelled of lilacs, which love our cold climate. Feeling exuberant, we decided that we needed a block party, and we quickly worked up an invitation and sent it to all twenty-two homes on our dead-end street.

We chose a day in June specifically because that would be before any really hot weather set in. Well, that day turned out to be the hottest of the summer—a blazing 98°—absolutely unheard of in northern Vermont in June. But we held the party anyway, and put out a sprinkler for the kids, which they thought was a wonderfully original idea since they are country children used to lake swimming.

After this get-together, we embarked upon another neighborhood project. The town had just finished paving our dirt road, and several of us decided that we were tired of grass and gravel driveways, so we formed a group, got estimates, and hired one company to do seven driveways—and saved quite a bit of money.

We have all come to know each other better and mutual help has become the norm on our street. During the 1998 ice storm, for example, we all checked up on each other constantly. I particularly appreciated that because I live alone.

We cooperated in other ways. My next-door neighbor was the only one on the block with a gas stove, so we all took turns cooking at her house. No one had a functioning oven, however, and as I watched an ap-

ple pie slowly defrost in my freezer, I called several friends in nearby towns and finally found one who had electricity. After a neighbor helped me disconnect my heavy garage door from its electric motor and lift it by hand, I drove the pie to my friend's house and baked it.

By this time everyone had become interested in my pie because we were planning a party to eat up all the defrosting food in the neighborhood. It was a great evening with the wildest, most varied menu that anyone had ever seen—consumed by candlelight. Our cooperation in normal times made much more intense teamwork possible during a crisis.

One evening, in fact, after we heard that a favorite pizza house had electricity, fourteen of us hopped in three cars and ate a communal meal together. Then, having acquired a taste for warmth, we went to the local cineplex, which also had power. I can tell you that enjoying a friendly relationship with your neighbors is more than pleasurable—it is healthy, because it gives you a sense of security. You know your place in the community and feel as though you belong. Dr. Douglass Carmichael, who is a consultant to the U.S. Department of State, Director of Critical Humanities Institute (www.tmn.com/y2k), and one of the world's wisest Y2K thinkers, points out that crisis sometimes brings out the best in people because a shared purpose brings us together. He says that in times of crisis people display unparalleled levels of creativity and resourcefulness, a desire to help others, and leadership behaviors, which appear everywhere as needed. People also learn and respond with lightning speed and experiment constantly to figure out what works.

You are probably sick of ice storm stories by now but we have to include one more. A man who lives in the next town loaned fifteen generators to neighbors and farmers who had lost power. When power was restored, he picked up his generators, loaded them into his truck, and drove for over an hour to a hard-hit section of Grand Isle County that was still without power, offering them to those in need.

For many people, however, frequent moving is the norm, and this can make it difficult to become part of a community. In fact, according to a biannual survey conducted by the National Board of Realtors, Americans change homes about every seven years. New jobs due to the reconfiguration of the work force in specific locations, military transfers, and retirement cause a great deal of relocation, making mobility a reality of American life.

So it is not always easy to know your neighbors. Also, human nature being what it is, when you get to know them, it is impossible to like everyone. Even if you are new to a community, it is a good idea to find a core of people in your neighborhood with whom you get along, because the quality of your relationship with these families could affect your experience during a natural disaster or Y2K emergency.

Alerting Your Neighborhood

It is important that you alert your neighbors to possible millennium emergencies, and what you are doing to prepare for them, because a prepared neighborhood is much more likely to come through any problems in good, cooperative shape. You don't want to be in the position of having the only supply of food and water on your block, and having to deny your neighbors help because you have only enough for your own family.

But be sure to do this in a low-key way. If you sound too excited or conjure up doomsday Y2K scenarios, your neighbors may think that you are mildly demented. We suggest, if you choose to discuss it with the folks on your block, that you mention it quietly. If someone responds with interest by saying, "Oh, yes, we heard such and such the other day, and isn't it true that this might happen under certain situations," then this is a person with whom you can discuss these issues. Pass along a copy of this book. If, on the other hand, your neighbor draws a total blank at the mention of Year 2000 computer problems, don't push it. You might, however, suggest that you consider it an important issue and if they do hear anything on the radio, or read anything in the papers, that they pay attention to it, because you would be interested in hearing what they think about the matter. If you sense interest in the neighborhood, arrange a meeting or potluck to discuss the matter, and, if there is enough interest, schedule a larger meeting by posting flyers around town or putting an ad in the local newspaper.

Organizing Community Response

The broader community, of course, provides schools, police and fire protection, emergency services, local ordinances governing everything from traffic to taxes, and essential municipal services, such as water supply, sewage disposal, garbage collection, and operation of the local landfill. The potential challenges at the municipal level from the Y2K bug, as in natural disasters, are legion. The millennium bug poses all the same risks to the community that it does to the home, most notably power failures, which would affect all municipal functions, including water purification and distribution. What happens if the fire department finds no pressure in the water main? Or the phones are out and you cannot call the dispatcher to get an ambulance or fire engine when you need it?

The opportunity to imagine catastrophe may greatly exceed the actual disaster when it arrives. However, the regrettable fact is that significant leaders, including Senator Robert Bennett, chairman of the U.S. Senate Special Committee on the Year 2000 Technology Problem, and John Koskinen, the White House's Y2K Czar, are saying that we do not know what will happen on January 1, 2000 and for a period of time thereafter. Senator Bennett said in July 1998, "It is clear we can't solve the whole problem, so we have to allow some systems to die so that mission-critical systems can work." He went on to point out that he expected the power grid to function, with some brownouts and regional blackouts, phone and financial services to be available, and most areas to have clean water.

With so much uncertainty expressed at such a high level, prudent municipal leadership should develop. In addition to a standard natural emergency preparedness plan, every community needs a Y2K-preparedness plan that will—at the very least—create resilient shelters to meet the basic needs of citizens who have failed to make adequate preparations in their own homes. We need to recognize that there are millions of people in our country, particularly in dense and poor urban areas, who will find it challenging, perhaps impossible, to become Y2K-ready in any meaningful way. These people will not be able to withstand infrastructure disruption for more than a few days.

To organize an intelligent Y2K response, Norfolk, Nebraska, invited Dr. Carmichael to a town meeting on Y2K issues, co-sponsored by the town council and community college and run by the city administrator. The meeting was attended by two hundred people: official representatives of local corporations (including the primary supermarket), Nebraska Public Power, and U.S. West Bank, as well as members of the police, fire, water, and sewer departments. After discussion of the millennium bug and its possible impacts, Carmichael said, "Time is short and I need your leadership to help us get organized." The entire group outlined the topics requiring attention and one hundred and twenty people signed up for fourteen groups. A meeting of the heads of the groups will plan the next town meeting, which will be open to the whole town and the surrounding communities. Said Carmichael,

> It was American Democracy right out of de Toqueville, and a great model for others. It is quite simple. The key is to keep sponsorship of the meeting open, not to let it be ideological, allow the townspeople to set up the categories for the meeting groups they want, and to frame it as an increase in infrastructure which increases the capacity of the town to respond to Y2K. It obviously moves beyond the normal lines of officialdom, which is beautiful and essential.

In Lubbock, Texas (population 186,000), the business and agricultural hub of the South Plains, a committee of town employees assigned to prepare a Y2K drill modeled various millennium failures on paper, which they gave to city officials to get an idea of how they would respond. One problem the model sought to answer was whether the local power company would function in the event of computer failures in other parts of the national power grid. The answer was "No." As a result, the city plans to stockpile one million gallons of diesel fuel before December 31, 1999, which power company officials feel is enough to run the plants until power from the national grid is restored. Mayor Windy Sitton explained the drill as "characteristic of [the city] as a whole. We tend to take care of ourselves [in Lubbock]. We're aware that we are remote. We know we have to depend on ourselves."

A Prepared Community

One community that has prepared for the millennium bug is Bethlehem, New York, a town of twenty-eight thousand that serves as a bedroom community for the Albany area. The town supervisor, Sheila Fuller, is a gung-ho lady who was just becoming aware of possible computer bugs when she received a call from town resident Norman Kurland at the end of 1997, asking if she was aware of the Y2K problem. Kurland, who is involved with the very active Y2K group in Albany, offered to meet with her and her department heads. Together they looked at all services—water, sewer, fire, police—their emergency management plan, and their computers. Fuller and her managers appreciated Kurland's help and soon she had the programmers on staff going through endless lines of computer code to make the dates compatible with a four-digit year 2000. This didn't take too long because they had relatively new equipment. So Town Supervisor Fuller feels confident that Bethlehem will be up and running on January 1, 2000.

But, and there always seems to be a but, it is another story concerning the companies that supply services to the town. For example, Niagara Mohawk, Bethlehem's power company, is going through a restructuring. The company has said, in response to a letter from Fuller, that it is working on a Y2K-compliance plan, but Fuller isn't sure how much progress has been made. She has also written to the phone company and, at Kurland's suggestion, to the managers of all the supermarkets in town, but, at this writing, she has not yet received replies.

As for emergency services, emergency personnel have a plan in place that would work for Y2K, which was established and perfected after the town suffered through ten days without power in 1987 because of a massive snowstorm. The town hall and all schools automatically become shelters in an emergency.

Fuller believes most people are ignoring the problem. As a result, she held a public meeting in the fall of 1998, and plans another one this year. The Bethlehem Chamber of Commerce has been alerting all businesses, large and small, so people should gradually become aware of the millennium bug.

Action You Can Take in Your Community

The unfortunate reality is that many communities have barely begun to consider the Y2K problem, let alone to prepare plans or take action. This situation is beginning to shift. In March 1998, Dermot asked the mayor of a fair-sized city his opinion about Y2K. At the time, he did not take the issue seriously. As of January 1999, however, the mayor is addressing the issue, and taking a real leadership role.

As an ordinary citizen, you can bring to the attention of community officials your considered opinion on important municipal and community matters, one of which surely is the problems that may arise because of the Y2K bug. Write to your mayor, or call city hall or your town selectboard, and ask specifically who is leading the effort to create a Y2K-preparedness plan. The person responsible is probably the same individual who developed your town's emergency response plan for natural disasters. Even though Y2K is a human-made problem, the skills needed to respond to any disaster are the same.

Write or speak to the person in charge of Y2K preparedness. First, find out what he or she is doing to make sure those services your home depends on—water, sewage, and sanitation—will continue in the event of Y2K disruptions in your area. Second, ask what is being done to assure that your community's police and emergency services can continue to function despite Y2K disruptions.

Listen to the planner's response and determine if you are dealing with a knowledgeable person who has been taken seriously by the mayor's office and the heads of the municipal departments. If there is any reason you are less than satisfied with the answers, you may have to take further action.

That means writing to the city council or town selectboard and the mayor, and sending copies of your letter to the local newspaper. Visit the mayor's office and talk about the issue, always confronting the mayor in a friendly, nonaggressive way. Do the same with the department heads providing essential services that you and your family depend on for the continued enjoyment of your home.

If you meet with resistance, flag the relevant portions of this book, including this chapter, and give it to the people responsible for your town's smooth functioning. Tell them that during the ice storm of 1998 in the northeast, thirty thousand people left their homes and sought refuge in shelters because they were not prepared to survive without power. And that number is only the tip of the refugee iceberg, because scores of people who could afford it sought refuge in specially discounted hotel rooms; many others stayed with friends or relatives. Point out that in the event of a worst-case Y2K scenario, which many thoughtful and intelligent people have suggested could happen, citizens would be likely to hold them responsible for the lack of municipal services.

If you are concerned that the powers-that-be in your town are not doing enough, become more active and attend a meeting of the citizen governing body, where you can raise the issue. Find out if community leaders are organizing any meetings to deal with the Y2K issue and attend them. If they are not, you may have to become a leader and organize a grassroots effort.

Getting Outside Help

If you need help in your community endeavors, visit the Cassandra Project on the internet at www.millennia-bcs.com (for the frames version) or www.millennia-bcs.com/nfcass.htm (for the no-frames version). Cassandra, in myth, always told the truth but was never believed. A grassroots nonprofit organization and winner of the 1998 Social Innovations Award, the Cassandra Project wants to raise public awareness and alert public sector organizations of potential Y2K-related health and safety risks involving possible interruptions of basic and essential services. The Project tries to promote community preparation activities; monitor federal, state, and local Y2K activity that relates to public welfare; and promote contingency planning for all health, safety, and essential services. It encourages the public to ask elected officials to develop health and safety contingency plans and has established a clearinghouse for related information and contacts. The site has an index of articles and resources, a list of Year 2000 problems that have already occurred, and covers other topics, including banking, the economy, embedded chips, communications, energy, health, the military, personal finance, law enforcement, water and sewage issues, and the activities of federal agencies. It is trying to promote community with a capital "C," and is setting a course that many communities should follow if they don't want to suffer when the new millennium arrives.

CHAPTER 11

RESILIENCE VERSUS VULNERABILITY

I'd say pay attention to those things that are vulnerable in your life
and try to get a contingency plan for them.

SENATOR BOB BENNETT,
*chairman of the U.S. Senate Special Committee
on the Year 2000 Technology Problem,
speaking to the National Press Club, July 15, 1998*

 IN THIS CHAPTER, WE WANT TO TALK ABOUT THE practical costs of preparing for Y2K. First, though, it will be useful to look at examples of how some people have already made the transition to resilience.

Resilience at its most comfortable and best integrated level is a lifestyle choice. We call it the resilient lifestyle. It is created not out of or in response to fear, but instead it is the product of a mature and reasoned observation that the ways of the world are subject to occasional interruption. The resilient homeowner consumes less, tends toward the simple rather than the complex, enjoys all the conveniences of the world in moderation, and is not helpless when the bubble of constant supply has been pricked.

Following are two examples of resilient homeowners. Libby Doherty's life and home is a fine example of simple living, resilient enough to sustain itself for a long time when the external supply lines to her home are disrupted for any reason. Further along the spectrum of resilience, Don and Valerie Schroeder's house is entirely independent of the utility grid. Bob Zylinski's house occupies the functional space between these two poles. We hope that these examples will awaken your imagination to the possibility and promise of the resilient lifestyle.

Libby's Home

Libby Doherty lives in a resilient home. Its resilience is as much conveyed by the lifestyle of its owner as it is the components of the home. The house is simple, well rooted in the land. It is a small three-story structure, sheltered with an earth berm on the northern side of the first floor. To block the cold winter winds, Libby and her husband (now deceased) planted trees, which are now full grown, on the north side of the house. The kitchen is on the first floor, and it has as its center a wood-fueled cooking range that also provides domestic hot water and radiates heat into the room. The kettle is on the hob, reminiscent of rural Ireland where the kettle is always on the boil ready to "wet the tea." In the dry winter air of Vermont, the kettle helps humidify the home. A hot-water coil at the back of the kitchen range provides heat to the water tank. Libby says that this doesn't provide great amounts of hot water, but does provide some. The tea that she makes her guests is from herbs, such as chamomile, grown in her garden and dried by hanging from the ceiling beams of her kitchen.

On the second and third floors, Libby has wood stoves connected to the central masonry fireplace, which in turn provides thermal mass for better distribution of wood heat. The orientation and windows allow the gain of some solar heat and brighten her home.

Libby is an avid gardener. She plants and harvests her garden with care, and clearly enjoys producing and using as much food as she can from her own garden. Her dietary habits focus on locally available food, to the point that, in response to a passing reference to rice, she pointed out that it doesn't grow in Vermont. She also enjoys eggs, courtesy of the chickens that she keeps.

She depends upon a well for her water supply. Near the well is a 1,000-gallon water cistern system that she and her husband put in years ago. It has not been used in years, but she is considering cleaning it out and using the cistern as a water storage facility in case of need.

Libby enjoys the conveniences provided by her local electric utility, but she also has a backup generator. Recently, her daughter and grand-

child came to live with her, and the generator was useful during a week-long regional electric outage. Many of her neighbors had to leave their homes for at least part of the 1998 ice storm because their homes lacked resilience.

Libby's home has a quality that is hard to capture in a written narrative. This is what we mean when we say the house is rooted in the land. There is an easy, comfortable relationship between the home, the kitchen garden, the woodpile, the chicken coop, the well, and the surrounding land. The home is imbued with its own sense of grace, woven into the home by the lifetime of routines and patterns that Libby has established. She is now in her eighties, slowing down a bit perhaps, and she continues to enjoy living in her own resilient home.

Libby's home is prepared for outages caused by Y2K and weather-related events, but it was never Libby's particular intent to prepare her home out of fear of such events. Rather, her home is resilient out of choice. This is the opportunity that Y2K presents to us: To reassess the way in which we live and to adapt to sustainable habits and patterns that will bring simplicity and harmony into our lives.

Bob's House

Bob Zylinski is a single parent with two children. Bob, a renewable energy enthusiast, looked for a strong reason and a comfortable enough bank balance to finally take the plunge into renewable energy. His work as a technician in an electronic products facility, combined with personal experience of an electrical outage, gave him the final impetus to plan and install a renewable energy system. He hired Kirk Herander of Vermont Solar Engineering to do the work.

For heating, Bob relies on both an oil furnace and a wood stove. Since he has a resilient heating system, his primary concern was to have enough home-generated electricity to provide a reliable supply of well water and one or two electric lights during a power outage. The basis of his system is a battery/inverter charged by the electrical utility. The battery system includes four 220-amp golf cart type batteries, wired to produce 24 volts. In a full state of charge, with a voltage of about 25 volts, this battery bank will store 5,500 watt hours. The one-half HP well pump draws the most electricity, consuming about 800 to 1,000 watts when running. Under routine use, the well pump will operate for about fifteen minutes a day. Without any additional charge, the batteries provide a twenty-day supply of well water without any curtailment of use. The batteries are vented to the outdoors, a crucial element to prevent the buildup of dangerous and explosive gases. A 2,400-watt inverter supplies power to the well pump and other small domestic loads. Herander estimates that the batteries will last a lot longer than the average three to five years, because Bob uses them only during electrical outages.

To maintain the batteries in charge during outages, and for regular use, Bob has a small 300-watt wind generator and a small two-panel 150-watt solar electric array. Even in the worst winter months, these two sources provide an ample supply of charging current to meet all the critical needs of his home. A few years before installing the wind turbine, he installed an anenometer (a wind measuring device) to determine the best site for a wind generator on his property. This took six months.

The entire system cost approximately $6,000, including all control features, the transfer switch to protect the renewable energy system from the electric utility current, lightning protection and grounding, as well as the costs of installation. The system has lots of redundancy for meeting critical loads. Those in sunnier climates might choose to go with two or three photoelectric modules and forgo the wind generator. Likewise, those in dark northern environments with good wind exposure might forgo the solar modules, and focus instead on the wind generator. Admittedly, for a backup system, this is expensive. Still, we want to encourage those who can afford it, and who would enjoy the opportunity to work with renewable energy, to go ahead and install such a system. The alternate way to provide for critical electrical needs in times of disruption would be to purchase a standby electrical generator, which, if of the highest quality, could cost nearly as much as a renewable energy system, and which, of course, requires a frequent supply of fuel. Wouldn't it be a delight not to add to the potential Y2K-inspired gasoline lines?

The Schroeder Home

On a hill in the town of Colchester, Vermont, not far from Burlington, stands a brand new house that looks like many others but is a world apart from most contemporary homes. The owners are Don and Valerie Schroeder, an attractive couple with two young children. Their dream has been to build a house totally independent of the energy grid, and the fact that Don is a master electrician who can do his own electrical work, and can trade his services with colleagues in the building trades, has brought the cost of the expensive technology he used low enough to make their dream a reality.

What kind of electrician builds a house that is not connected to any power company? Someone who values independence and conservation. The Schroeders are practical folks who believe in using that which is free—the power of the Sun and the wind. Despite the cloudy Vermont winters, Don started with one simple fact: you can use the Sun when it shines to create electricity, and you can store it for later use in a large battery bank in the basement. Thus this house uses solar panels not only to produce electricity for power and storage but also to run the solar hot water heater. When there isn't enough power, the Schroeder's backup energy source is a propane-powered generator. A control panel and inverter manages the distribution of power and switches from one source to the other automatically. In addition, a wood stove in the living room takes advantage of a renewable energy source and keeps the house warm as toast in winter. Don installed a one kilowatt Whisper 1000 wind generator in the fall of 1998 to create more power and cut down on their propane use. The generator sits atop a tower 98 feet high, located 200 feet from the house. This addition cost $2,000 for the generator and an equal amount for the installation. "But," says Valerie, "the wind is free." The Whisper requires slightly more maintenance than the solar panels do; once every few years it needs to be taken down to have its bearings checked.

Does the house look any different than the average home? Not in the least. There is a mud room at the entry; a large modern kitchen and open dining area; a living room with comfortable upholstered furniture, the wood stove, and a TV; a study shared by Valerie and Don; three upstairs bedrooms and two baths, one of which has a large jacuzzi tub next to the window. The appliances are run-of-the-mill; in fact, by not spending a fortune to buy appliances recommended in solar publications, the Schroeders saved enough money to pay for the wind generator installation. You would not know there was anything different about this house unless you went down to the basement and saw the batteries, inverter, and other special equipment required to store and disperse energy from the solar panels and the wind and propane-powered generators, or unless you went looking for an electric meter on the outside of the house or a bill from the local power company.

The joys of energy independence became apparent during the ice storm in January 1998. Valerie remembers that they didn't know there was a problem until they turned on the TV for the evening news and heard about the blackout. "I remember looking out that afternoon and thinking how pretty it was with all the tree limbs glazed and sparkling. Of course, once I knew, I immediately roasted a big turkey and called several friends to join us for dinner the next day." Throughout the five days of the storm, friends and relatives dropped by to cook, take showers, get warm, and hear the news. The Schroeders were great people to know when ice decided to coat Vermont and turn off all the power.

Most people will not go out and build a new energy independent house, though if you plan to, you could consider the Schroeder approach. But everyone may be able to take bits and pieces of the Schroeders' overall plan to increase their independence of the power grid. Installing a wood stove is one easy and effective option. Alternately, it is possible to buy a battery/inverter electric-storage setup, charge it while the power grid is running, and then use the stored energy to run some of your appliances during a temporary power failure or as backup during the rolling blackouts that some experts predict will happen as the result of Y2K problems. Bev is investigating installing a solar panel on her deeply pitched roof, since it faces south, to create enough energy to power a battery that will run her well pump during the next blackout. In short, there are many good ideas out there, both for conserving energy and taking advantage of the energy the Sun and wind freely supply. The secret is a new kind of thinking that embraces the concept of energy independence.

The Cost of Resilience

Now we come to the nitty-gritty of the whole Y2K business. If you've read this far, you probably agree that the year 2000 requires some preparation. But you may also be saying to yourself, "Do I really have to do all this? Where will I find the time to research all the options and decide which are best for my home? And, most important, what will resilience cost me? Can I afford it?"

The better question might be, can you afford to do nothing? The costs of contingency solutions range widely. Coping with power failures can be as simple as having on hand a half-dozen flashlights, a dozen multiple battery packs to power them, a couple of kerosene lamps, and a hefty supply of candles; or as involved as deciding that it is necessary to purchase a generator to run several crucial appliances, and the computer in your home office. Having enough water can be as simple as filling every large soda bottle your family has finished to buying top-of-the-line containers and easy-to-use water packets. Your family's extra food supply can consist of the simplest fare, or you can prepare or buy gourmet specialties. Alternative heat can come from a simple wood or gas-powered stove, or from a solar panel system and large battery to store excess power. The choices are many, but we hope that you will choose the most Earth-friendly technology.

Remember that these contingency plans apply not only to the Year 2000, but to any natural disaster as well. Bev would have given a great deal during the 1998 ice storm for a hand pump for her well, or a generator to run the electric one, for the absence of clean water was her greatest problem. Preparing a home for possible Year 2000 emergencies and the fury of nature increases its value—when you sell it, its resilience can be an important selling point.

Finally, it is not just money involved here; it is peace of mind. Clearly it is better to be pleasantly warm in winter, not freezing; pleasantly cool in summer, not boiling over; well fed, not famished; relaxed and secure, not worried and frustrated. Maybe it can't be measured in cash, but there is definite value attached to being prepared for emergencies—which is good for your physical and mental health.

Our final advice to you is to choose those options that fit your particular home and budget (use the table on pp. 152–53), and spend time in 1999 making sure you have established a viable contingency plan for your family. Once you have a Y2K-prepared home, you can—as flight attendants always advise—sit back, relax, and enjoy the ride.

Estimated Expenses for
A Y2K-prepared Home

Heating

Wood @ $110/chord	$6/Million BTU
Coal @ $139/ton	$6/Million BTU
Natural Gas @ .65/therm	$10/Million BTU
Pellet @ $185/ton	$13/Million BTU
Propane @ .99/gal	$16/Million BTU
Electricity @ .08/kWh	$24/Million BTU
Woodstoves	$600–2,000
Fireplace inserts (without installation)	$1,600–2,100
Hearth requirements for wood stove (without installation)	$300–800
Flue for woodstove	$800–1,200
Masonry chimney installation for wood stove	$3,000
Cord of wood	$100–140
Solar submersible pump kit	$1,500
Wind generator (large)	$8,000–16,000
(small)	$1,200–2,000

Heating with Gas

Gas fireplace (without installation or mantel)	$1,000–2,100
Decorative gas space heater	$1,200–2,100
Non-decorative space heaters	$975–1,250
Direct vent for gas fireplace or space heater (decorative & non-decorative)	$200–400
Hearth requirement for gas space heaters (decorative & non-decorative	$0–200
1,000-gallon propane tank	$0–1,200

Batteries/Inverters and Generators

Transfer switch	$500–700
Fossil fuel generator	$400–1,000
Bifuel generator	$1,600
Trifuel generator	$4,000
UPS device (Uninterrupted Power Supply)	$89–500+
Kits to battery/inverter system	$750–2,000

Battery/inverter packs
  2 kWh storage $780
  8 kWh storage $2,000

Natural Cooling
  Custom-made square-type fabric awning
    fitting a window up to 5' wide $180–450
  Conventional aluminum fixed awning $100–300
  Aluminum awnings with movable louvers $160–400
  Retractable awning 10–40 feet wide $1,500–5,000
  Roll-down curtain $4–4.50 per sq.ft.
  Bahama shutter, top-hinged $220–250

Food
  MREs (12 full meal packs) $69/case
  Emergency food bars (90) $69.95/case

Water and Sanitation
  hand pumps for deep wells $500–800
  hand pumps for shallow wells (or sump pump)
    Sigma $120
    Guzzler $48–60
  Pitcher pump $60
  water sachets, case of 60 packets $14.95
  Instantaneous tankless hot water heater $640–700
  Ion (2-ounce bottle) $14.95
  Composting toilets $1,000–1,300
  Cadillac model composting toilet $2,500

RESURCES

Heating, Cooling, and Lighting

Alpha American Company
1000 Ag. Science Drive
P.O. Box 20
Palisade, MN 56469
800-358-0060
www.alphaamerican.com
(multi-fuel furnaces)

Awnair
419 Jessen Lane
Wando, SC 29492
888-881-1197
www.awnair.com
(window awnings)

Chimney Sweep Fireplace Shop
3113 Shelburne Road
Shelburne, VT 05482
802-985-4900

Ecological Innovations1
4 Tech Circle
Natick, MA 01760-1086
800-876-0660

Enterprise
73 Lorne Street
Sackville, New Brunswick E4L 4A2
www.enterprise-fawcett.com
email: enterpri@nbnet.nb.ca
(Canada only; electric-free oil space
heaters)

Gentran
P.O. Box 8
Waukesha, WI 53187
414-544-4811
(automatic and manual transfer
switches)

Green Lights
U.S. Environmental Protection
    Agency
401 M. Street SW (62021)
Washington, DC 20460
202-775-6650

Heatmor Outdoor Furnaces
Highway 11E Box 787
Warroad, MN 56763
800-834-7552
www.heatmor.com

American Honda Motor Co., Inc.
4475 River Green Parkway
Duluth, GA 30096
800-426-7701
www.honda.com
(generators)

Jade Mountain, Inc.
P.O. Box 4616
Boulder, CO 80306-4616
800-442-1972
www.jademountain.com

Lehmans
One Lehman's Circle, P.O. Box 41
Kidron, OH 44636
330-857-5757
www.lehmans.com
email: getinfo@lehmans.com
(Aladdin kerosine lamps)

National Association of Energy
  Service Companies
1440 New York Avenue
NW Washington, DC 20005
202-371-7980

Newmac Manufacturing Inc.
P.O. Box 9
Debert, Nova Scotia BOM 1GO
800-565-3840
www.Newmacfurnaces.com
email: newmac@fox.nstn.ca
(Furnaces: oil, gas, solid fuel and
multi-fuel)

Perfection Schwank
P.O. Box 749
Waynesboro, GA 30830
www.psheat.com
(electric free oil space heaters)

Real Goods
555 Leslie Street
Ukiah, CA 95482-5507
800-762-7325

Rising Sun Enterprises, Inc.
P.O. Box 1728
40 Sunset Dr. #1
Basalt, CO 81621
970-927-8051

Rocky Mountain Institute
1739 Snowmass Creek Road

Snowmass, CO 81654-9199
www.rmi.org
(renewable energy)

Seventh Generation
49 Hercules Drive
Colchester, VT 05446
800-456-1177

Slant/Fin Heating and Air
  Conditioning Equipment
100 Forest Drive
Greenvale, NY 11548
516-484-2600

Solar Depot
61 Paul Drive
San Rafael, CA 94903
800-822-4041; 415-499-1330
www.solardepot.com

Superia
US Department of Energy
Office of Technical Support
P.O. Box 62
Oak Ridge, TN 37831
423-576-2286 or 576-8401
www.ornl.gov/roofs+walls
www.erendoe.gov
(vent free heaters)

Winco Inc.
225 S. Cordova Avenue
Le Center, MN 56057
507-357-6821
(generators)

Yamaha Motor Corporation
6555 Katella Avenue
Cypress, CA 90630
800-692-6242
www.yamaha-motor.com
(generators)

Food, Water, and Health

American Waterworks Association
(AWWA)
700 Cardinal
Elgin, TX 78621
512-285-2770

Aquacheck
1300 West Pioneer Street
Suite C
Brear, CA 92821
800-504-5580; 714-739-7755
(MRE's, Emergency Food Bars, water
sachets)

Bosworth Company
930 Waterman Avenue
E. Providence RI 02914-1337
888-438-1110; 401-438-1110
(hand pumps)

Energy Federation Incorporation
14 Tech Circle
Natick, MA 01760-1086
800-876-0660; 508-653-4299
www.efi.org
(carbon monoxide detectors)

Gardener's Supply
128 Intervale Road
Burlington, VT 05401
800-863-1700

Monitor
133 Enterprise Street
Evansville, WI 53536
608-882-2721
(hand pumps)

National Gardening Association
180 Flynn Avenue

Burlington, VT 05401
800-538-7476
www.garden.org

National Ground Water Association
601 Dempsey Rd.
Westerville, OH 43081
800-551-7379
www.ngwa.org

Rintoul's Hand Pumps
1225 Dorcas Bay Rd., RR #2
Tobermory, ON NOH 2RO
519-596-2612
www.handpumps.com
e-mail: handpump@kanservu.ca

USDA Office of Communications
Room 536 A
1400 Independence Ave. SW
Washington, DC 20250-1300
www.ocio.usda.gov/y2k/techcon.htm

Walton Feed
800-269-8563
www.waltonfeed.com/ion4.html

Water Wiser
6666 West Quincy Avenue
Denver, CO 80235
800-559-9855
www.waterwiser.org
(resource for water efficiency)

Money, Transportation, and Communication

American Power Conversion
800-800-4272
www.apcc.com/template/size/
workstation/single/intl/
(to determine UPS requirement)

Chelsea Green Publishing Company
P.O. Box 428, 205 Gates Building
White River Junction, VT 05001
800-639-4099; 802-295-6300
(books for sustainable living)

Federal Deposit Insurance
    Corporation (FDIC)
www.fdic.gov/about/y2k
(Y2K issues)

Intel-based PC BIOS Test for Year
    2000 Problems
www.gatech.edu/year2000/
biostest.htm

IBM Technical Support Center,
Year 2000
www.software.ibm.com/year2000

Microsoft Year 2000 Resource Center
www.microsoft.com/year2000

PC & Mac Connection
Rt. 101A, 730 Milford Road
Merrimack, NH 03055
800-800-5555
www.pcconnection.com
(UPS devices)

Vendor and Specific Product
Readiness Info
www.vendor2000.com
(with search capability)

Community

Association of Minnesota Counties
www.mncounties.org/year2000.htm
(provides an annotated list of links to
other sites about Y2K)

Dr. Douglass Carmichael
www.tmn.com/y2k

Cassandra Project
www.millennia-bcs.com

League of Minnesota Cities
www.lmnc.org/public/yr2000/
LMCYR2000.htm
(includes a downloadable 72-page
Year 2000 Action Guide for cities)

Lowell Massachusetts Y2K Preparation
www.lowellonline.org/bna/y2k/

Napa Valley California
www.y2knapa.com/

Northern Virginia Y2K Community
    Action Group
www.novay2k.org

Rick Ingrasci
Community Resilience
www.y2kcommunity.org

Santa Cruz California;
Draft document for Y2K Community
Planning
www.cointelligence.org/
y2k_communityplan2.html

Helpful websites

Congressional Y2K Sites
www.itpolicy.gsa.gov/mks/yr2000/
us.htm#congress
www.itaa.org/congress.htm

Rick Cowles
www.euy2k.com

Emergency preparedness tools &
accessories
www.theepicenter.com/toolacc.
html#radio

GAO (General Accounting Office)
Y2K Reports
www.gao.gov/y2kr.htm

General Services Administration
(GSA) Act S2392, introduced by
Senators Leahy and Hatch
www.itpolicy.gsa.gov/mks/yr2000/
y2khome.htm

House Committee on Science
Subcommittee on Technology
www.house.gov/science/y2k.htm

International Information Directory;
links to other countries' Year 2000
Web sites
www.itpolicy.gsa.gov/mks/yr2000/
g7yr2000.htm

International Y2K Conference
www.itpolicy.gsa.gov/mks/yr2000/
y2kconf/g7conf.htm

Nuclear Regulatory Commission
www.nrc.gov

President's Council on the Year 2000
Conversion
www.y2k.gov
Public Technology Inc.
www.pti.org

Senator Bob Bennett of Utah
Chair of Senate Committee on
Year 2000 Technology Problem
www.senate.gov/~bennett

Special Senate Committee on The
Year 2000 Technology Problem
www.senate.gov/~y2k/index.htmlt

Summary of daily Y2K news
www.cruxnet.com/~sanger/y2k/

U.S. Government Gateway for Year
2000 Information Directories
www.itpolicy.gsa.gov/mks/yr2000//
y2khome.htm

Dr. Ed Yardeni Economic Network
http://Yardeni.com

Y2K for Kids
www.litpolicy.gsa.gov/mks/yr2000/
kidsy2k.htm

Year 2000 articles
www.year2000.com/articles/
articles.com

Year 2000 Information Center
Peter deJager
www.year2000.com

Westergaard Year 2000 site
www.y2ktimebomb.com

➤ BIBLIOGRAPHY

Ausubel, Kenny. *Restoring the Earth: Visionary Solutions from the Bioneers.* Tiburon, Calif.: H.J. Kramer, 1997.

Burns, Max. *Cottage Water Systems.* Buffalo, N.Y.: Cottage Life, Inc., 1995.

Campbell, Stu. *The Home Water Supply: How to Find, Filter, Store and Conserve Water.* Pownal, Vt.: Storey Books, 1983.

Coleman, Eliot. *Four-Season Harvest.* White River Jct, Vt.: Chelsea Green Publishing, 1992.

Evangelista, Anita. *How to Live Without Electricity and Like It.* Port Townsend, Wash.: Loompanics Unlimited, 1997.

Hawken Paul. *The Ecology of Commerce.* New York: Harper Collins, 1993.

Jenkins, J.C. *The Humanure Handbook.* Grove City, Penn.: Jenkins Publishing, 1996.

Jones, Capers. "Year 200 Contingency Planning for Municipal Governments." www.angelfire.com/mn/inforest/capersj989.html. U.K.

Kachadorian, James. *The Passive Solar House.* White River Jct., Vt.: Chelsea Green Publishing, 1997.

Laddon, Judy, Tom Atlee, and Larry Shook. *Awakening: The Upside of Y2K.* Spokane, Wash.: The Printed Word, 1998.

LaLiberté, Katherine, and Ben Watson. *Passport to Gardening.* White River Jct., Vt.: Chelsea Green Publishing, 1997.

Moffat, Anne Simon, and Mark Schiler. *Energy-Efficient and Environmental Landscaping.* South Newfane, Vt.: Appropriate Solutions Press, 1994.

Pace, Arnold, and Adrian Cullis. *Rainwater Harvesting: The Collection of Rainfall and Runoff in Rural Areas*. London, U.K.: Intermediate Technology, 1986.

Potts, Michael. *The Independent Home: Living Well with Power from the Sun, Wind, and Water*. White River Jct., Vt.: Chelsea Green Publishing, 1993.

Roseland, Mark. *Towards Sustainable Communities Resources for Cities and Their Governments*. Gabriola Island, B.C.: New Society Publishers, 1998.

Schaeffer, John. *Solar Living Sourcebook*. White River Jct., Vt.: Chelsea Green Publishing, 1996.

Stevens, James Talmage. *Making the Best of Basics*. Seattle, Wash.: Goldleaf Press, 1997.

Van Der Ryn, Sim, *The Toilet Papers*. Sausalito, Calif.: Ecological Design Press, 1978.

Weisman, Alan. *Gaviotas: A Village to Reinvent the World*. White River Jct., Vt.: Chelsea Green Publishing, 1998.

Yourdin, Edward, and Jennifer Yourdin. *Time Bomb 2000: What the Computer Crisis Means to You*. Upper Saddle River, N.J.: Prentice Hall, 1998.

INDEX

CHELSEA GREEN

Sustainable living has many facets. Chelsea Green's celebration of the sustainable arts has led us to publish trend-setting books about organic gardening, solar electricity and renewable energy, innovative building techniques, regenerative forestry, local and bioregional democracy, and whole foods. The company's published works, while intensely practical, are also entertaining and inspirational, demonstrating that an ecological approach to life is consistent with producing beautiful, eloquent, and useful books, videos, and audio cassettes.

For more information about Chelsea Green, or to request a free catalog, call toll-free (800) 639-4099, or write to us at P.O. Box 428, White River Junction, Vermont 05001. Visit our website at www.chelseagreen.com.

Chelsea Green's titles include:

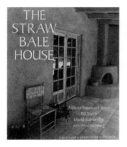 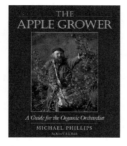 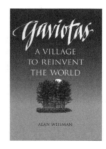

The Straw Bale House
The Independent Home:
    Living Well with Power
    from the Sun, Wind,
    and Water
Independent Builder:
    Designing & Building a
    House Your Own Way
The Rammed Earth House
The Passive Solar House
The Sauna
Wind Power for Home &
    Business
The Solar Living Sourcebook
A Shelter Sketchbook
Mortgage-Free!
Hammer. Nail. Wood.

The Apple Grower
The Flower Farmer
Passport to Gardening:
    A Sourcebook for the
    21st-Century
The New Organic Grower
Four-Season Harvest
Solar Gardening
Straight-Ahead Organic
The Contrary Farmer
The Contrary Farmer's
    Invitation to Gardening
Forest Gardening
Whole Foods Companion
Simple Food for the
    Good Life
Keeping Food Fresh

Gaviotas: A Village to
    Reinvent the World
Who Owns the Sun?
Global Spin:
    The Corporate Assault
    on Environmentalism
Hemp Horizons
A Patch of Eden
A Place in the Sun
Renewables are Ready
Beyond the Limits
Loving and Leaving the
    Good Life
The Man Who Planted Trees
The Northern Forest